Train Stations of the World

Martin Weltner

Train Stations of the World

From Spectacular Metropolises to Provincial Towns

4880 Lower Valley Road • Atglen, PA 19310

TABLE OF CONTENTS

Foreword __ 6

Train Stations—Introduction __ 7

I. Europe—It All Started in England __ 15

II. Africa—Continent of Contrasts __ 101

III. Asia and the Middle East—Great Diversity __ 127

IV. Australia and New Zealand—More than Just *Lord of the Rings* and Koalas __ 161

V. The Americas—a Journey from North to South __ 167

Photograph on page 2:

The track layout and station building at the main railroad station in the Gundeldingen district of Basel, Switzerland. | picture alliance / ZB / euro-luftbild

▶ The Simplon Express with steam engine A 3/5 703 in the Geneva train station, taken in 1906. Geneva was connected to the railroad network as early as 1858. | picture alliance / Keystone

FOREWORD

It has been almost 200 years since the world's first railroad station was built in Darlington, England, thus making it possible for the traveling public to use a new means of transport. This first station has little in common with the transport stations springing up all over the world today along the new high-speed rail lines, which offer much more than just access to the train. Modern train stations are often more like shopping centers. In some aspects, they are becoming like modern-day airports, with large waiting areas. Yet, what all train stations have in common is that they still have great appeal for many people, because they are places for departures and farewells, arrivals, and the joy of seeing someone again. Train stations can become routine; anyone who travels daily to work through a magnificent station may soon fail to appreciate it. And commuters using rural or small-town railroad stations are likely to be annoyed by delays or lack of service. Nevertheless, train stations offer the prospect of an escape from everyday life; when boarding your train, you have a distant destination in mind.

This book explores railroad stations on five continents—modern, functional buildings; old and new metropolitan train stations that are architectural masterpieces; and also small country train stations that rarely see a train or passenger. Many of the aerial photographs show the railroad stations from a perspective that is not available to ordinary passengers; it is all the more fascinating when you see "your" station from a completely different point of view. I wish you much enjoyment in reading, studying the photos, and becoming absorbed in the details that make so many train stations worth a good look. And last but not least, this illustrated book makes it possible to take an exciting mental journey around the world.

Martin Weltner

TRAIN STATIONS—INTRODUCTION

"I'm going to quickly go and pick up Grandma from the train station." How often have you said or heard this sentence yourself? It raises this question: What actually is a train or railroad station? For Germans, the Railroad Construction and Operating Regulations, "Eisenbahn-Bau- und Betriebsordnung (EBO), answer this question quite clearly: "Railroad stations are railroad facilities with at least one switch, where trains may start, end, enter a siding, or terminate. The entry signals or *Trapeztafeln* (trapezoidal boards), which are used in German railroad stations in general, constitute the boundary between the railroad stations and the open track; otherwise, it is the *Einfahrweiche* (entry switches)." A station's definition is regulated in a similar way in other places, but for this illustrated book we will consider the term "train station" or "railroad station" somewhat more broadly, and we also include stopping points and way stations. Have you ever heard someone say they are going to pick up Grandma at the train stop?

How do we distinguish train stations from each other? First of all, it is a question of the station's location in the network, its layout, and its function within a railroad network. Terminal train stations (also called railheads) are among the most impressive stations because they are often older and architecturally charming. In a terminal station (colloquially also a terminus), the main tracks dead-end at a buffer stop. The station building often stands at the end of the tracks. In older structures in particular, there is a crossover or a rail turntable or wheelhouse at the end of the tracks, making it possible to turn the traction units and move them to the other end of the train. Terminal train stations are often found in large cities; they date from the early period of railroad construction and were built to bring the railroad as close as possible to the city center. Many cities have several terminal stations serving a number of railroad companies that made their ways to the metropolis from all directions.

The most common type of railroad station, however, is the through station. In these stations, the main tracks of one or more rail lines run through the station area, link to track connections there, and, if necessary, are extended by additional station tracks. One type of station design widely used in the United States is the combined terminus-and-through railroad station; some of the tracks are station tracks with platforms that end at a buffer stop, while others are through tracks that allow the trains to run on through the station. Another American specialty should be mentioned: most of the terminal stations are connected with triangular junctions.

The main station in Dresden, Germany, seen from the perspective of a guest at the Kaisercafé, located opposite. This tinted photograph was taken at the turn of the twentieth century. There was already a streetcar system to provide "modern local transport." | picture alliance / arkivi

The Rentzschmühle train station in Vogtland, Switzerland, is located on the Gera Süd-Weischlitz line and is now served by the Vogtland Railroad. This historical photograph shows a stylized steam train standing by the ornately decorated train station ensemble (left). The light-colored building to the left of the train is likely a railroader's house. | picture alliance / arkivi

Incoming trains did not roll into the terminal station, which usually had a large train shed; rather, they would first roll into the triangular junction and then be pushed backward into the station. Why make all this effort? To avoid having the steam locomotives drive into the train shed and possibly fill it with smoke. This practice was maintained in the diesel age—too much diesel smoke isn't good for your health either!

In terms of distinguishing a station by its location in the network, first we have the terminal station, which is at the end of one or more railroad lines. The most common type of station is the intermediate station, a place for rail services along a through route. Then there are junction and connecting stations: At a junction station, there is at least one line branching off, while in contrast to a connecting station, the trains are able to cross from one line to the other. A connecting station, or feeder line station, has at least one other line branching off, but no regular through-train service. As a rule, the line that branches off is clearly the secondary line. Thus, classic connecting stations are mainline railroad stations from which local service lines branch off.

An interchange or transfer rail station has at least two lines crossing. If several lines meet there, it is a hub or central station. What's rarer are so-called "contact" train stations (*Berührungsbahnhöfe* in German), where two lines meet without crossing each other. However, local tracks often connect the two.

As already noted, station buildings are usually located to the side of the railroad facilities or, in a terminal station, crosswise to the tracks where they end. There are a few interesting exceptions, such as the "over-track"-type stations, called rider railroad stations (*Reiterbahnhof* in German), where the station building sits above and over the tracks. Another special facility is called a wedge railroad station (*Keilbahnhof* in German). At these stations, several rail lines diverge at the platform area. The station building, which has an almost triangular floor plan, sits between the diverging rail lines, which form a wedge. A characteristic feature of "island" railroad stations is the position of the station building, which is located on an island surrounded by the tracks on all sides. In a two-level interchange station, called a tower station (*Turmbahnhof* in German), there are at least two rail lines, but there is no level crossing. The lines cross each other at distinctly different levels. In larger two-level interchange stations, building a curved train station makes it possible to provide train service between the two levels of the station. The very rare triangular railroad station (*Dreiecksbahnhof*) provides an additional connection between the branching lines.

View of the main waiting room, or concourse, in the Chicago & North Western Station, which was built between 1908 and 1911 to replace many smaller train stations. In addition to the C&NW, other railroad companies also used this terminus, designed by the Chicago architects Frost & Granger. It was demolished in 1984 after the widespread decline of US passenger rail service. | picture alliance / Glasshouse Images

▶ This tinted postcard shows the Bellinzona train station in Ticino, Switzerland, before the railroads were electrified in 1920. Opened in 1874, the Bellinzona Railroad Station on the Gotthard Railroad and the Ticino Valley Railroad is today the largest railroad junction in the canton of Ticino. To the right of the tracks you can see the station buildings, including the roofed platforms; in the foreground are the railroad yard or depot facilities, including the engine house, which has been expanded several times. | picture alliance / ullstein bild

Now let's take a brief look at the history and development of stations. From the very first years of the railroads, station buildings were functional, modest affairs. For example, stations along the first German railroad from Nuremberg to Fürth were largely built of wood. But just a few years later, more-elaborate train stations began appearing. In the second half of the nineteenth century, they developed into imposing places with public appeal and represented the railroad companies themselves. Railroad companies had reason to celebrate themselves: the railroads stood for progress, and they were an economic success. Among the larger stations were waiting areas for special passengers; there were "royal railroad stations" and "imperial rooms." But there was no skimping on smaller train stations either. By the end of the century, increasing rail traffic had outgrown the capacity of railroad facilities built in the mid-nineteenth century. In addition, city centers were expanding exponentially, and the old railroad facilities were in the way of development. The buildings were replaced or the entire station moved to outer city limits. Another sensible option was to combine the stations of various railroad companies into a new one. Due to the end of the

The first railroad station on a connecting line to the Moscow–Vladivostok Trans-Siberian Railway was located in front of the Beijing city wall. This photograph, taken around 1910, does not show much activity going on; there are only a few goods being loaded, shown in the foreground. | picture alliance / ullstein bild

rail boom that followed World War I and the industry competition that emerged shortly after, train station design became focused on operational efficiency. This led to eliminating the terminal stations, which increasingly represented an obstacle as rail transport became faster and the locomotives switched from steam to diesel and electric. As a result, terminal stations were replaced by new buildings; the most recent example is the Berliner Hauptbahnhof (Berlin Main Railroad Station), along with plans for Stuttgart 21 and Lindau 21—new through railroad stations.

The decades after World War II brought a decline in railroad station culture. In addition to decay, in some places new buildings of questionable architectural, structural, or service quality were erected, and historical buildings were not valued. In rural areas especially, train stations became visibly dilapidated after the rail lines were abandoned. Railroad companies are not always able to find buyers for defunct station buildings, or any profitable way to reuse them. Many station

This photograph of Grand Central Terminal in New York City dates from the 1920s. This terminal station in the borough of Manhattan is one of the biggest train stations in the world; its sixty-seven tracks end at forty-four platforms on two levels, and it is still of great importance today, above all for suburban transport. The building has been carefully modernized several times without losing its classic character. In another unique feature, the Waldorf Astoria Hotel has its own platform in the terminal. | Everett Historical / Shutterstock

Union Station was built in Washington, DC, in 1907; here it is shown immediately after it was opened. Mighty signal gantries dominate the picture; behind them, many covered platforms can be seen, as well as a shadowy view of the terminal building. A steam train is ready to depart, and the exit signal has already been pulled out from the switch house, which also served as the viewpoint for taking the photograph. | Everett Historical / Shutterstock

buildings lost their ability to function, even on rail lines that were still in use, when a train station was downgraded to simply a stopping point as new technology was installed and machines took over ticket sales. In the last few years, only a few new large-scale station buildings have been built as part of the conventional railroad network. Among other things, this book will present the new main train stations in Berlin and Vienna. New, architecturally ambitious train stations on high-speed rail lines are being constructed around the world, and they almost always accommodate extensive shopping facilities. Today, railroad stations earn money for their operators above all as a commercial property, and not simply as a transport station.

I. EUROPE— IT ALL STARTED IN ENGLAND

Great Britain is rightly considered the motherland of the railroad. As early as 1825, the first passenger trains were operating between the towns of Stockton and Darlington, and five years later the Liverpool and Manchester Railway began running a service between those two major cities. Hundreds of private railroad companies consolidated the railroad network in the following decades, and train stations sprang up everywhere, from small country stations to imposing station buildings in medium-sized and large cities. Competition among the railroads resulted in ever more pompous buildings intended to court the goodwill of the traveling public. British train stations typically have elevated platforms; these made it possible to eliminate the steps needed to board passenger coaches. Even the smallest stations have such platforms, which are built mostly of masonry. After numerous railroad mergers, the British Rail national railroad was established in 1948. British Rail closed competing lines and unprofitable branch lines. However, in the last few decades, many lines have been making a comeback, taken over by railroad enthusiasts and put back into service—usually powered by steam locomotives. Particular attention was paid to restoring the old stopping points and train stations, including the signal systems. In some cases, new buildings even replicated historical models.

London—Great Britain

King's Cross, in the borough of Camden, is one of London's main train stations. Opened in 1852 by the private Great Northern Railway, this terminus provides long-distance service to northeastern England and eastern Scotland via the East Coast Mainline. Between 2008 and 2012, King's Cross was completely renovated. The station concourse was redeveloped, and a semicircular ticket hall was built, which can be seen in the middle of this picture taken in 2018. The main train shed has special meaning for Harry Potter fans: this is where the train to Hogwarts departs. | picture alliance / Heritage Images

15

◀ **London—Great Britain**

Not far from the river Thames—also called the Isis along some stretches of the river—is London Bridge Station, which consists of a terminus, a through station, and a London Underground station. London Bridge is the oldest train station in the British capital. The first terminal station in the facility opened in 1836; after several renovations and expansions, the train shed was built in 1866 and is still standing. Trains first started arriving here when it was a through station in 1864. From 2012 onward, station development continued. Its six through and nine terminal platforms have now become nine through and six terminal platforms, increasing the station's capacity. There are no electrical contact lines in London Bridge Station; the tracks in the station and the tracks for the outgoing lines are electrified with the traction current system common in southern England (lateral conductor rail with 750 V direct current). This photograph shows the station in 2008.
| picture alliance / Construction Photography

▲ **London—Great Britain**

View into King's Cross Station from the terminal station concourse with long-distance trains ready to depart. There are three multiple-unit trains of the private rail operator London North Eastern Railway (formerly Virgin Trains East Coast). To the left and right are two class 91 power cars; in the middle is a classic class 43 diesel multiple unit—Virgin Trains took over the vehicles in 2015 from the previous rail operator, East Coast.
| Dmitry Tkachenko Photo/Shutterstock.com

▶ **London—Great Britain**

A view into the semicircular ticket hall at King's Cross Station. From here, the train platforms, the Underground (the Tube), and the connected St Pancras train station can be reached a short distance away. The London system of platform barriers ensures that departing passengers can reach the platforms via the upper floor of the new concourse and the new pedestrian bridges, while arriving passengers leave the building at ground level via the concourse.
| Aniczkania/Shutterstock.com

Europe 17

London—Great Britain

Liverpool Street Station is one of the many terminal stations in London, the metropolis on the Thames. Besides Waterloo and Victoria, it is one of the busiest train stations in London, with around seventy million passengers a year. Liverpool Street serves destinations to the east, including the port of Harwich, where there are ferry connections to continental Europe. The express service to low-cost Stansted Airport also leaves from Liverpool Street. The station went into full operation in 1875; previously some suburban trains had already started arriving there. Yet, the station soon became too small and was significantly expanded starting in 1888. The station was badly damaged by German bombers during World War I, with hundreds of dead and injured recorded. In the following decades, the station repeatedly reached its capacity limit, but this did not result in any major conversions or additions. Instead, effective reorganization measures were carried out. Structural neglect necessitated renovation in stages between 1973 and 1991. While the original plan was to demolish the station and replace it with a new building, public protests resulted in the western train shed's restoration and reinforcement. Extensive rebuilding of the tracks was deemed impractical, but a more efficient signal system was installed, which meant that the nearby Broad Street station could be abandoned.
| picture alliance / picture agency-online/Joko

Llangollen—Great Britain

Llangollen is a picturesque town in northern Wales. From here you can easily reach Snowdonia, the extraordinarily beautiful mountainous region and national park. The railroad found its way here when the Vale of Llangollen Railway was built in 1861, but after roughly a hundred years of service, this line connecting the towns of Ruabon and Bala was closed down. Railroad enthusiasts saved a section of the route and in 1975 began to run it as a heritage railroad with historical steam and diesel locomotives. Today, it is once again possible to travel a 12 km long section running from Llangollen along the River Dee valley to the town of Corwen by train. | CloudVisual/Shutterstock

Brighton—Great Britain

The roof of the Brighton Station train shed gleams in its filigree-like quality. The station building, which still stands, was planned by the architect David Mocatta (1806–1882) in Italian Renaissance style and was opened in 1841 with a line to the town of Shoreham. In 1882–83, the station was expanded considerably. The imposing platform concourse and the roofing over the station forecourt were built at the same time. During 1999–2000, the train shed was extensively renovated and its blue paint color was restored.
| Marius_Comanescu/Shutterstock

Brighton—Great Britain

It was the dead of winter in Great Britain on February 27, 2018, when this local train pulled into London Road station in Brighton. The unadorned suburban station is on the East Coastway Line, operated by Southern (the Govia Thameslink Railway). This line connects Brighton with Lewes, Eastbourne, Hastings, Ore and Ashford, and other destinations. | Marius_Comanescu/Shutterstock

Weybourne—Great Britain

The British heritage railroads are considered to be the most beautiful in the world, and rightly so! The Weybourne train station on the North Norfolk Railway, which has been lovingly restored and spruced up, is shown here as a photographic freight train is passing through on June 12, 2014. The train's locomotive is an English Electric Class 37 D6732 diesel locomotive, which was called a "Mirage" during the times of British Rail. Heritage railroad enthusiasts keep it running. | Kev Gregory / Shutterstock

Gravesend—Great Britain

Gravesend is located in the county of Kent, and its railroad station is less than 40 km from the London Charing Cross station. The first trains began stopping here in 1845; today the station is connected to London by local and intercity services. In 2013, the station was renovated from the ground up, and today it is a modern transport station with three canopied platforms. It is used by more than three million travelers each year. Only the station building in the foreground recalls former times. This photograph from 2018 shows a multiple-unit train of the private rail operator Thameslink ready for departure to London. If the name Gravesend sounds familiar, it might be because Pocahontas died here in 1671 and was laid to rest in St George's Church. |
Flyby Photography / Shutterstock

▶ **Glasgow—Great Britain**

All the signals in the Glasgow Central train station were red on October 25, 2000, and the glittering tracks were empty. The background to this blockade was the serious accident that occurred on October 17. Four people were killed and at least seventy were injured when a high-speed train derailed on an elongated curve near Hatfield in Hertfordshire. The privatized British railroad company Railtrack admitted that the accident was caused by a fragmented rail. The condition of the track system was described as "completely unacceptable." At the time, Railtrack unleashed complete chaos in Britain's rail traffic by closing the most important line running to northern Great Britain. The route was closed for three days without any warning so that the tracks could be examined for possible cracks.
| picture alliance / dpa

◀ **Glasgow—Great Britain**

Glasgow Central Station, which opened in 1879, is the Scottish city's largest train station. This terminal station has been making a colorful impression since the British railroad system was privatized. This photograph shows a Virgin Trains multiple-unit train standing next to one belonging to the CrossCountry railroad company, a subsidiary of Germany's Deutsche Bahn AG railroad company. On the far right is a passenger coach in the Scotrail design. Scotrail operates the largest portion of the passenger train service in Scotland. |
picture alliance / prisma

◀ **Inverness—Great Britain**

Inverness, population 50,000, is on the river Ness in the Highlands of northern Scotland. The city is shown here in bird's-eye view. The railroad facilities, which form a large triangle of tracks, are clearly seen, along with the main train station and its train sheds with platforms to the north. The first railroad line reached Inverness from the town of Nairn in 1855. More rail lines followed, until the line westward to Kyle of Lochalsh was completed in 1897. The terminal railroad station has seven station tracks with platforms, and five of these extend into the main train shed. ScotRail handles most of the train service. The Caledonian Sleeper is a special feature; the train offers a sleeper-only service, providing a comfortable overnight way to travel to London six times a week. It runs on the West Coast Main Line. | picture alliance / ZB / euroluftbild.de

Edinburgh—Great Britain

Edinburgh Waverley is the main train station of the Scottish capital city and is squeezed between Edinburgh's Old Town and New Town in a kind of moat. This photograph shows the two station tracks, with platforms located outside the train shed. Access to the trains running on the sixteen additional tracks is provided inside the train shed to the left. Seen in the background, the North Bridge spans the through-station facilities. The palatial Balmoral Hotel in typical Victorian architecture can be seen to the left The hotel's clock is always set two minutes fast so that passengers will not miss their trains. | picture alliance / Exss

Europe **27**

◀ **Dublin—Republic of Ireland**

The main building of Dublin Connolly Station has been a protected historical landmark for years. Built between 1840 and 1850, it was initially called Dublin Station and was later renamed the Amiens Street Station after the construction of additional terminal stations in Dublin. It was given its current name in 1966 in honor of James Connolly, who was executed for his participation in the 1916 Easter Rising. Today the train station has seven station tracks with platforms, four terminal tracks, and three electrified through tracks. These are used mainly by local DART (Dublin Area Rapid Transit) trains. | picture alliance / imageBROKER

Portadown—Northern Ireland, United Kingdom

You will find this typical Northern Ireland provincial train station in Portadown in County Armagh. The railroad station is equipped with elevated platforms, and the station building can be seen on the left. The passenger has access to the central platform via a steel pedestrian bridge; in the foreground, a small water tower serves as a reminder of the era of steam locomotives. A DMU, which stands for diesel multiple-unit train, sits ready for departure at the platform by the station building. The United Kingdom has been acquiring these multiple-unit trains, powered by onboard diesel engines, in umpteen different designs since the 1950s for running the rail service on branch lines. | picture alliance / Construction Photography

▲ Mora—Sweden

Mora is a small town with around 10,000 inhabitants in the Swedish province of Dalarna. It lies on Lake Siljan and is therefore a popular tourist destination. Mora can be reached by train from Stockholm via Uppsala. It is also the southern terminus of the Swedish Inlandsbanan (Inland Railroad), which runs northward to the town of Östersund in central Sweden and on to Gällivare in the far north. The train station—a typical Scandinavian wooden structure—is shown in well-kept condition in February 2015. The passengers have long been allowed to leave the waiting room and find their places in the electric railcar, which stands ready to depart on the platform.
| Michael715/Shutterstock

◄ Gällivare—Sweden

With only around 10,000 inhabitants, Gällivare, north of the Arctic Circle in Lapland, is only a small town. Yet, it has not only a railroad connection, but one that lies on a European route highway (part of the international E-road network) and can also be reached by air. Gällivare is important as a transportation hub for the Luleå–Gällivare–Kiruna–Narvik Iron Ore railroad and the Swedish Inland Railroad, which terminates here. The train station, built in the log house style, was once given an award as the most beautiful train station in Sweden.
| Göran Sandström, CC BY 4.0

The railroad network in Scandinavia is not very dense, particularly in the northerly regions. One of its special features is the broad-gauge tracks used in Finland, compared to the trains run on standard-gauge tracks in Denmark, Sweden, and Norway. (Broad-gauge tracks are 1,668 millimeters [mm] wide, or 5 feet, 5.6 inches, while standard gauge is 1,435 mm or 4 feet, 8.5 inches).

The tidy, wooden train station buildings are typical of the Scandinavian countries—in forest-rich countries, this simply makes sense. The distance between the stations is quite long, especially in sparsely populated areas, and train service is limited. Accordingly, most train stations have spacious waiting rooms, which are heated as needed, making the time spent waiting for the train a pleasant experience.

Gothenburg—Sweden

The "blue hour" in Gothenburg (Göteborg), Sweden's second-largest city with around one million inhabitants. In the foreground you can see the track system at Gothenburg Central Station, a terminal station with sixteen tracks. It is possible to reach all the major cities in Sweden from this electrified train station, and there are international connections to Oslo and Copenhagen, among other cities. Urban rapid-transit trains are used for local transport. The world's first electronic interlocking system was put into operation in Gothenburg Central as early as 1978. There are future plans for a railroad tunnel running beneath the city to provide Gothenburg Central with two through tracks. | Henryk Sadura / Shutterstock

Sochi—Russia

The Russian city of Sochi, which lies on the Black Sea, hosted the 2014 Winter Olympics. To make the trip there convenient and attractive, this new modernist Sochi Olympic Park railroad station was built not far from the Olympic Park. The three platform canopies, stacked one higher than the next, are as impressive as the curved-glass roofing. In 2016 the station's name was changed to Imeretinsky Kurort. This city, at the foot of the Caucasus Mountains, has an eventful history. It came under the rule of the Russian tsar after the Russo-Turkish War of 1828–1829. Before that, it had been under Ottoman rule for several centuries. | Zotov Dmitrii / Shutterstock

The railroads of Russia—who doesn't think of the famous Trans-Siberian Railroad, the main transport axis of Asiatic Russia and, with its 9,288 kilometers (km), the longest single railroad line in the world. Running along the entire route from the Russian capital of Moscow to the port of Vladivostok on the Pacific coast, the tracks pass 400 railroad stations, a trip that takes six days. The rail networks in the former Eastern Bloc countries, from Poland to Bulgaria, are far more European in character. During the last few decades, a large amount of money has been invested in the railroads, but at the same time, many lines were shut down in the face of increased competition from road traffic. Many train stations have been modernized, such as the Prague Main Railroad Station, and other stations are still waiting for an extensive renovation, such as those in Romania and Bulgaria.

Petrozavodsk—Russia

Petrozavodsk is the capital city of the Russian republic of Karelia, roughly 400 km northeast of St. Petersburg. Petrozavodsk Central Station lies on the Murmansk Railroad, which runs from St. Petersburg to the port city of Murmansk. It was hastily built between 1915 and 1917 because of its great strategic importance during World War I. This photograph shows a passenger train, hauled by a Russian EP 1 class electric locomotive, ready to depart The station building with its tower and spire, including the Soviet-era star, is visible behind the trees. | picture alliance / Johannes Glöckner

Europe 33

◄ Lviv—Ukraine

In 1861, the (imperial Austrian) Galician Railway of Archduke Charles Louis built the first train station in Lviv, Ukraine. (Lviv was known as Lwów under Polish rule and called Lemberg, or Lviv, during the Austro-Hungarian Empire in the former region of Galicia). This building was replaced by a new station west of the city center, which was opened in 1904. Parallel to the through-station building, two massive train sheds display the typical steel-and-glass architecture of the time. They were rebuilt after being destroyed during World War II. Shown here is the outermost of the two train sheds; the support structures on the left side of the picture also support the inner train shed, which is connected to the train station building. | Pavlo Lys / Shutterstock

Warsaw—Poland

The Szybka Kolej Miejska w Warszawie (SKM Warszawa, City Rapid Rail) has been operating an urban rapid-transit system with four lines in greater Warsaw—the capital of Poland—since 2005. The Falenica train station in the far southeast of the city, shown from a bird's-eye view in this photograph, is on SKM Line 1, which runs between the towns of Pruszków and Otwock. Next to the station building platform, which like the center platform has a wide canopy, stands a modern Class 35WE "Impuls" multiple-unit train made by the Polish manufacturer Newag, which is based in Nowy Sącz in southern Poland. | Bartosz Dziugiel / Shutterstock

▲ **Bucharest—Romania**

A still life at the Bucharest North Railway Station, with waiting passengers and a Romanian railroad electrical veteran. While the interior of the station building has been renovated with European Union funds, there is still a lot of work to be done on the train platforms. | Vlad Ispas / Shutterstock

Bucharest—Romania

The Bucharest North Station, the main train station of the Romanian capital city, is an impressive facility. This terminus with fourteen tracks was built between 1868 and 1872 and is the largest train station in Romania. The station is important not only for local transport but also for long-distance service, since almost all long-distance Romanian trains start or end at Bucharest North. In this photograph you can clearly see the enormous length of the station tracks with platforms. The passenger trains, each with seven or eight cars, are almost lost in the station.
| Augustin Lazaroiu / Shutterstock

Prague—Czech Republic

The Prague Main Railroad Station, listed in the timetable under Praha hlavní nádraží, is the most important long-distance train station in the Czech capital and the largest passenger train station in the country. This through station lies east of the city center and has rail connections to most of the other Prague train stations. The train shed has two hall bays. The bays house a station building platform and three island platforms, as well as seven tracks with platforms and one set of locomotive tracks. Three more island platforms serving six station tracks are located outside the train shed; these are protected with individual roofs. In addition, there are three terminal tracks, two on the southern side and one on the northern side. Opened in 1871, the railroad station was given its current station building between 1901 and 1909. | M-SUR/Shutterstock

The picture on the right shows the impressive art nouveau entrance hall of the train station. | Thomas Ledl, CC BY-SA 4.0

Prague—Czech Republic

The striking and magnificent station building is clearly visible in this aerial photograph of the Prague Main Railroad Station. The art nouveau building was built between 1901 and 1909 and designed by architect Josef Fanta, using sections of the first station building, which was built in 1871. In the process of constructing the Prague subway system around 1970, the main station was given a new, two-part entrance hall, partially built into the slope. This can be seen in the foreground. The roof area of this hall is used as a parking deck, and the Wilsonova expressway runs above it. The entrances to the platforms for subway line C, which started service in 1974, are located in the first section of the entrance hall, with the ticket counters behind them. Stairs lead to the second section of the hall, primarily used as a waiting area. | Nadezda Murmakov / Shutterstock

Budapest—Hungary

The Keleti pályaudvar in Budapest (Keleti pu for short), or Eastern Railroad Station, is the largest of the three main stations in the Hungarian capital city. Originally, the trains were running to the east and southeast, serving the cities of Debrecen and Békéscsaba. Now, however, most international trains stop at this station, especially EuroCity trains traveling to Hungary. The station is also the terminal stop for Railjet connections from Munich, Zuric, and Vienna. This station can be reached via connecting lines from all the railroad lines leading to Budapest. The station building was designed in the neo-Renaissance style and was planned and built between 1881 and 1884 by the railroad engineer János Feketeházy and the architect Gyula Rochlitz. Since 2014, Keleti pu has also been a transfer point for the subway. The forecourt and parts of the station interior were rebuilt and renovated to accommodate those commuters. | Alexandr Medvedkov / Shutterstock

Vienna—Austria

The ultramodern Vienna Westbahnhof (West Train Station) is also known as a "shopping center with a railroad siding." As a result, you will find primarily shopping areas, offices, and service businesses in the building shown here, while the actual train station with its train shed, which is a protected historical landmark, is hidden behind the trees to the right. | Roman Plesky / Shutterstock

The history of the railroad in Austria began in 1824 with a horse-drawn tram that ran between the cities of Linz in Austria and České Budějovice, now in the Czech Republic. In the decades that followed, this country, whose size has changed several times due to wars and annexations, was opened up by means of a dense railroad network. There is a wide variety of architecture in Austrian railroad stations, often depending on which private railroad company built them. Thus, in the northern part of the country, for example, you can still find small, standardized local train stations, just as they were to be found along the once-numerous narrow-gauge rail lines. A lot of money has been invested in building new train station buildings in recent years; notable here are Linz station, Vienna's Westbahnhof, and, of course, the capital city's Hauptbahnhof (Central Station). At the same time, however, many branch lines were shut down, which led to the demolition or sale of charming branch line stations.

The Vienna Central Station, which opened in 2014, is on the site of the former Südbahnhof (South Station). Thanks to the new track connections, it is the first train station in Vienna to provide long-distance service in all directions, giving Vienna a functional central station for the first time in its history. The new station has five island platforms, located one level up, that are up to 450 m long, as well as two through tracks. The roofing over the platforms is an open design constructed in two halves. One half, the so-called diamond-shaped roof, consists of five rows of alternately sloping trapezoidal surfaces, as shown above. In each row, the roofs are half staggered to create a vertical opening between the roof surfaces.

These openings are glazed to fill the interior with light. One year after it opened, on December 13, 2015, the project's completion was celebrated. Since then, all ÖBB (Bundesbahn Österreich, or Austrian Federal Railways) long-distance service has been run from Vienna Central train station; the Westbahnhof, once the most important long-distance train station in Vienna, has become an important ÖBB regional train station for local service to and from the western part of the state of Lower Austria. | *Above left*: Sodel Vladyslav / Shutterstock. *Above right*: picture alliance / Karl Schöndorfer / picturedesk.com. *Below left*: picture alliance / Karl Schöndorfer / picturedesk.com. *Below right*: tolgaildun/Shutterstock

Europe **43**

▲ Schafbergspitze—Austria

Since 1893, a meter-gauge rack railroad has connected the town of St. Wolfgang, named for the lake it sits on, with the Schafbergspitze (Sheep Mountain Peak), 1,732 m above sea level. The train runs only in the summer season and is operated by steam and diesel locomotives. The maximum gradient along the route is 255:1000, and the trip takes a little more than thirty minutes. This photograph shows the modern mountain train station with two steam trains. The rack system—here an Abt system mechanism—installed between the rails of the two tracks can be clearly seen. Tourists (*far right*) are enjoying the view of Lake Wolfgang, which lies deep in the valley below. | Roman Kybus / Shutterstock

Hochschneeberg/Baumgartner—Austria

The local transport region of Vienna also features a rack railroad. This line runs from the town of Puchberg to the 1,796 m high Hochschneeberg mountain. The rail line's tracks are 1,000 mm broad, and, with a length of 9.7 km, it is the longest rack railroad in Austria. The colorful multiple-unit railcars (decorated to look like salamanders) are typical of the modern Schneeberg Railway; these railcars have been in service since 1999 and have largely replaced the old steam locomotives. This photograph shows two such railcars as they meet at the Baumgartner junction station, where a restaurant provides tourists with food and drink.
| Askolds Berovskis / Shutterstock

Berlin—Germany

One of the impressive sights of modern Berlin is the Hauptbahnhof, Berlin Central Station, which began operating in May 2006 and is the largest tower train station in Europe. The striking building was designed by the architect Meinhard von Gerkan. A new north–south railroad line running through a tunnel started service on May 28, 2006, realizing a complete reorganization of Berlin's rail passenger transport. When you look at how the lines run on a network map, this reorganized plan almost creates the visual impression of a mushroom, which is why the term "mushroom concept" (*Pilzkonzept*) has become part of the city vernacular. The area north of the Spreebogen (Spree River bend) was where the Lehrter Train Station stood from 1868 to 1951 and where the Lehrter City Train Station stood from 1882 to 2002. | Philipp Dase / Shutterstock

At one time in Germany, a station's style of architecture immediately gave away its regional location. Today this is less true. While regional-style stations still exist, such as the typical northern German brick buildings, many have been repurposed as residential buildings or tourist offices or are falling into ruin. The new station buildings no longer incorporate regional peculiarities; they are highly functional buildings that can also serve mobility-impaired travelers, for example. The metropolitan train stations, on the other hand, now often present themselves as "shopping centers with railroad services," with plenty of space dedicated to retail and gastronomy. This makes business sense, given that in the digital age there is no need for a large number of ticket counters, just as very large waiting rooms have also become generally obsolete thanks to fixed-interval train timetables. It is also significant that Deutsche Bahn (the German Railroad company) is increasingly abandoning the term Bahnhof ("train station" or "railroad station") and prefers to speak of Verkehrsstationen ("transport stations").

Berlin—Germany

The upper level of Berlin Central Station, which serves both long-distance and regional transport, is flooded with light; an IC (Intercity) train stands ready to depart on track 14. The upper track level consists of six tracks on four bridge structures. The two on the outer sides have single tracks, and the inner ones have two tracks each. In between, three platforms sit about 10 m above street level. The station surface area comprises 430 by 430 m. The centerpiece is an area of 80 by 80 m on which five distribution levels are arranged. The elevation difference between the top and bottom levels is 25 m. Fifty-four escalators, six panoramic elevators, ten additional elevators, and a range of stationary staircases connect the levels. | posteriori/Shutterstock

Europe 47

Berlin—Germany

The Friedrichstrasse train station is a Berlin classic. During the time when both Germany and Berlin were divided, this was the border-crossing station between West Berlin and East Berlin. The station is on the Stadtbahn—the urban train system—between Friedrichstrasse, the street of the same name, and the Spree River. Regional and city trains stop above ground at three platforms designated as A, B, and C from south to north. The platforms are on the urban rail viaduct and spanned by a larger train shed for the regional rail service and a smaller one for the S-Bahn, or Stadtschnellbahn, Berlin's urban rapid-transit system. After German reunification, the station was renovated and modernized; this included removing the structures at the border-crossing point. Deutsche Bahn invested 220 million deustch marks (DM) in the renovation of the former border train station. The facades were restored with glazed terra-cotta bricks, in keeping with the requirements of a protected historical landmark, and the south facade was clad in clinker brick for the first time. The 5,200 m² space contains fifty stores and other venues. | JJFarq / Shutterstock + picture alliance / imageBROKER

Bresewitz—Germany

The community of Bresewitz, in the municipality of Pruchten since 1974, is located at the entrance to the Darß Nature Reserve on the Baltic Sea coast. It sits in the middle of the Boddenneer—distinctive briny lagoons lying along Germany's Baltic Sea coast—near the city of Barth in the state of Mecklenburg-Vorpommern. The train station is located at the western edge and has not been in operation for a long time. The Darßbahn ("Darß train") ran through the town to the municipalities of Zingst and Prerow, but this line was dismantled after World War II. The tracks to the Bresewitz district were relaid during the 1960s and used by the East German National People's Army until 1990. The route of the tracks can still be seen clearly. Today the former train station houses vacation apartments.

| picture alliance / Maximilian Schönherr

Dresden—Germany

Dresden Hbf (Hauptbahnhof: Central Station) is the most important passenger station in the state capital of Saxony. Built in 1898, it is a rare example of a combined island station—with the station building on an island between the train tracks—and terminal station, which operates on two levels. The station has been rebuilt several times; it was badly damaged during World War II and finally completely renovated by 2000, although a 2002 flood damaged the new work. The renovated station was inaugurated beneath the dome of the station building concourse on November 10, 2006, the city's 800th anniversary. The opening marked the end of the major disruption to travel, but the renovation work, which also includes making individual platforms shorter, is ongoing. As is common today, many retail stores and restaurants have found their way into Dresden Central Station. | Alexandr Medvedkov / Shutterstock

Leipzig—Germany

View of the modernized platforms in Leipzig Central Station in December 2015, with IC (Intercity) and ICE (Intercity Express) trains. The keystone was laid on December 4, 1915, for the construction of what was once the largest terminal station in Europe, with its twenty-six station tracks with platforms. The passenger facilities were extensively renovated in the second half of the 1990s. This involved gutting the concourse area and the east and west corner buildings and inserting a shopping center with two additional floors below the concourse. Today the station building houses around 11,000 m^2 of rented premises with seventy-one shops. Twenty-four station tracks with platforms are available; one is used to exhibit historical rail vehicles. | picture alliance / ZB

Hamburg—Germany

A special feature of the Hamburg Central Station is the tracks that run in a gentle curve in the large train shed. Construction on this through railroad station began in 1904 and replaced the earlier scattered terminal train stations built by various railroad companies. It began operating on December 6, 1906. The train shed is 150 m long, 114 m wide, and up to 37 m high. The station building, flanked by two 45 m high towers with a square cross section, was built with a bridge or "north walkway" across the platform concourse on the north side. With daily long-distance and regional passenger services operating on just twelve tracks with platforms, this station is the biggest bottleneck in Deutsche Bahn's network, according to former rail boss Rüdiger Grube. In 2010, in response to a question from a member of Parliament, a federal official characterized the station as an "overloaded rail line." Incidentally, the Niebüll-Westerland (Sylt) line was added to this category in the same year.
| Riku Makela / Shutterstock

Frankfurt am Main—Germany

Night aerial view of the tracks and building of the Deutsche Bahn main station in Frankfurt am Main. In 1888, the station opened as the "Centralbahnhof Frankfurt"—Frankfurt Central Station. Originally, this terminus station had three train sheds, each with six station tracks with platforms; in 1924, two outer train sheds were added, blending in with the neoclassical ensemble. The number of tracks was increased to twenty-five. Between 2002 and 2006, the five platform concourses were renovated from the ground up, in compliance with historic-landmark regulations. In 2013, the station building facade was renovated, and the interior of the train shed and station concourses were modernized, as was the lower-level station for local train service. | picture alliance / ZB / euroluftbild.de

Blumenberg—Germany

Blumenberg station in the eastern state of Saxony-Anhalt is a small railroad junction on the main line between the cities of Magdeburg and Halberstadt, which has branch lines to Eilsleben, Schönebeck, and Stassfurt. In the years following German reunification, passenger service was reduced on all branch lines. Deutsche Bahn also abandoned the stop at Blumenberg for main line trains, due to low passenger volume. Shown here, in 2018, a railcar of the Harz-Elbe Express to Halberstadt is still running into Blumenberg station. Today it handles only a small amount of freight traffic and is at risk of being dismantled. Several mechanical signal boxes, semaphore signals, and a water tower from steam locomotive times remain in place next to the station exit toward Magdeburg. | Peter Gercke / dpa-Zentralbild / ZB

Mainz—Germany

Aerial photograph of Mainz Central Station, built between 1882 and 1884 as a through station. Constructed with sandstone in Italian neo-Renaissance style, between 1998 and 2000 the station was thoroughly modernized. Its concourse, dating from 1939, was replaced with a reinforced-concrete superstructure; the curving roof recalls the station's former train sheds. Today, countless ICE (Intercity Express), EC (Eurocity), and IC (Intercity) lines stop in Mainz, along with six RE (Regional Express), four RB (Regionalbahn (Regional Train Service), and two S-Bahn (urban rapid transit) lines. | picture alliance / ZB / euroluftbild

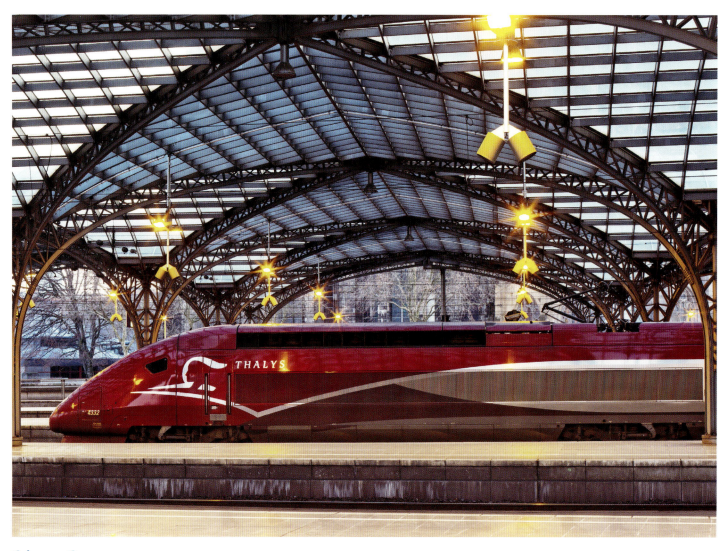

Cologne—Germany

The high-speed, multiple-unit trains of the French-Belgian rail operator Thalys are regular guests at Cologne Central Station and handle the high-speed service running in the direction of Belgium and France. Pictured is a PBKA-type multisystem train—the letters stand for Paris, Brussels, Köln (Cologne), and Amsterdam. Here, the train is standing under the architecturally striking platform canopy, facing southeast; the walls of Cologne Cathedral are visible in the background. Between 1989 and 1991, the platform canopy in front of the train shed and between the train shed and entrance hall was replaced with a design by Busmann + Haberer with Stefan Polónyi—architects of the neighboring Museum Ludwig. The train shed, itself a protected historical landmark, was extensively renovated. | Christian Mueller / Shutterstock

Cologne—Germany

Aerial view of Cologne Central Station and its impressive surroundings, including the world-famous cathedral (*right*) and the "Musical Dome" in front of the Hohenzollern Bridge. The bridge, which has been expanded several times to hold six tracks, connects to the Cologne Deutz Train Station on the left after it crosses the Rhine. Cologne got its first central station in 1857 but before long was unable to cope with the increased volume of rail traffic. In 1883, a new main station was built on the same site, although the tracks were elevated, along the lines of the Berlin Stadtbahn (city rapid rail service). Entire rows of houses were torn down to make way for the railroad.

In 1894, the large three-tiered train shed with platforms was completed, taking design cues from the train shed and platforms at London St Pancras station. With its span of 64 m, the longest at the time, the central train shed spanned what are now tracks 2 to 7; the two side train sheds, both 13.5 m wide, spanned tracks 1 and 8. In the course of building the S-Bahn, or urban rapid-transit system, until 1991, the entire railroad line, station, and Hohenzollern Bridge were expanded by adding two independent tracks. Two tracks (10 and 11) were added to the main station in 1975, and in 1989 the Hohenzollern Bridge with the S-Bahn main line was expanded to carry six tracks. | *picture alliance / dpa*

▲ **Dießen am Ammersee—Germany**

The Dießen train station is not far from the lovely Ammersee (Lake Ammer) in Upper Bavaria. It lies on the Ammerseebahn (Lake Ammer Railroad), which runs from the town of Mering via Geltendorf to Weilheim and was opened as a through station in 1898, after serving as the terminus for the line from Weilheim for a few months. East of the station building, a protected historic landmark in the Heimat (countryside) style, one can see the pier for the Ammersee ferry passenger boat service that connects Dießen with Herrsching on the east bank of the Ammersee. | picture alliance / Westend61

Munich—Germany

The Munich main train station is considered the transportation hub of southern Germany. It is a terminal station with thirty-two station tracks with platforms. Once known as the Centralbahnhof (Central Station), it has a long history. As early as 1848, the first trains ran to the site where today's main station stands. After suffering severe damage in World War II, the main train shed—shown in this photograph along with a Deutsche Bahn ICE (Intercity Express) train spanning platforms 11–26—was rebuilt in two phases, in 1950 and 1959–60. The train was 220 m long, significantly longer than earlier trains. In addition to the outer supports, which have a span of 70 m, it has a single row of central supports—an unusual design for the time. In addition to the main train shed, Munich Central also includes the Holzkirchener and the Starnberger wing stations. The station building, inaugurated in 1960, was demolished in 2019 to construct a second S-Bahn (urban rapid transit) tunnel. The new building is slated for completion by 2029. | Alberto Masnovo / Shutterstock

Augsburg—Germany

Railroad stations are places of continual change, as exemplified by the Augsburg Central Station—the terminal point of the busiest rail line in Germany (Munich–Augsburg). The first train station in the "city of the Fuggers"—a wealthy fifteenth- and sixteenth-century banking family—was built in a different place starting in 1838, not far from the city's Red Gate. This was also the terminal point of the rail line from Munich that started operating in 1840. Today it is part of a streetcar depot on Baumgartnerstrasse.

The station building of today's complex was built between 1843 and 1846. The architect was Eduard Rüber, who designed a number of train stations in Bavaria. Parts of the current iteration's slightly elevated middle section date back to this first building and its renovation a few years after completion. At another point in the nineteenth century, it was rebuilt and expanded, this time in the style of late classicism that was popular. The building remained unplastered, displaying its bare bricks until the 1930s. The building's appearance thus corresponded to that of many Bavarian "public buildings," such as barracks and post office buildings. Today, after minor alterations in the 1950s and modernization work from 1983 to 1984, the station is once again a major construction site: a tunnel is being dug beneath it to accommodate streetcars, and the new station will be barrier-free for travelers. The photo shows the construction work in full swing. | picture alliance / ZB / euroluftbild

Antwerp—Belgium

This photograph of the Antwerpen Centraal (Antwerp Central) railroad station in the center of downtown Antwerp, Belgium, was taken in March 2014. The compact-looking modern facility, dating from 1899 and 1905, has a 186 m long, 66 m wide steel train shed designed by engineer Clement Van Bogaert. Its impressive height of 43 m allowed smoke and fumes from the steam locomotives to escape. The stone station building (*center of the photo at the end of the train shed*) was designed in an eclectic style by Louis de la Censerie. He was inspired by the railroad station in Lucerne, Switzerland, and the Pantheon in Rome. Because of the dominating dome (75 m high), the building is popularly known as the "railroad cathedral." By the middle of the twentieth century, the train station was structurally compromised. Demolition was considered in the 1960s. Instead, it received historic-landmark status and was fully renovated beginning in 1993. | picture alliance / ZB / euroluftbild.de

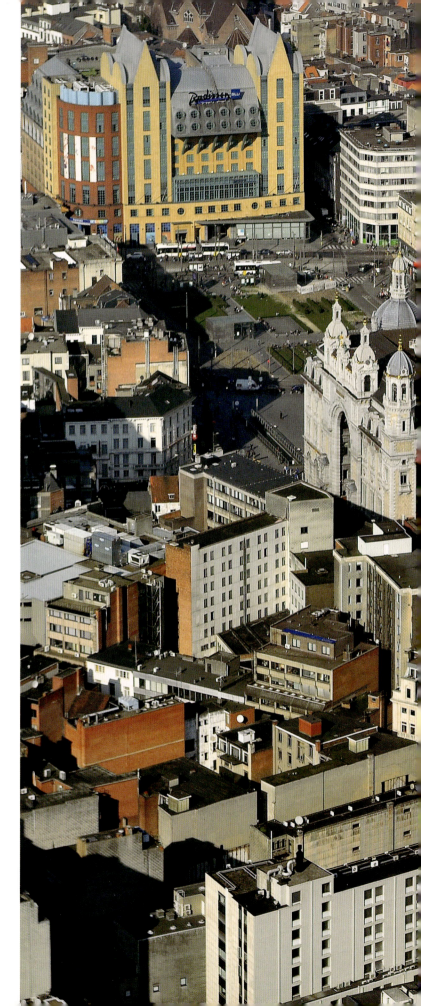

The Benelux countries of Belgium, the Netherlands, and Luxembourg have a dense rail network dating to the third decade of the nineteenth century. Incidentally, the Nederlandse Spoorwegen (Dutch State Railroad) stakes a claim to being the first in Europe to dispense with steam locomotives, in 1958. Today, the main lines in all three countries are fully electrified. Diesel multiple units have taken over transport services on branch lines still in operation. The most-important train stations in all three countries have been modernized in recent years or decades, so that they are able to meet the requirements of today's more frequent service. There are a number of heritage railroads that recall former railroading times. These feature not only interesting rail vehicles, but also lovingly restored and maintained infrastructure.

◀ **Utrecht—the Netherlands**

Utrecht Centraal station, popularly known as Utrecht CS, is the main train station in this Dutch city. It is the largest train station in the Netherlands, with eight platforms serving sixteen tracks. An initial railroad station had been built on this site in 1843, and frequent rebuilding and expansion work has occurred over the decades. Since 2008, the station and large parts of its surroundings have been completely rebuilt. A glass structure, designed by Benthem Crouwel, replaced the train shed, and the platform canopies are being renovated. The bus station, previously on the east side of the train station, has been divided to accommodate two bus stops. This aerial photograph was taken during reconstruction in June 2015. A year and a half later, a ceremonial opening celebrated the 420-million-euro renovation. Perhaps not surprising for the Netherlands, one of its most exemplary features is parking space for 12,500 bicycles. |
Aerovista Luchtfotografe / Shutterstock

Amsterdam—the Netherlands

A bird's-eye view of Amsterdam Centraal, the main train station of the Dutch capital city. Opening in 1889, the sprawling, neo-Renaissance-style station building was designed by architect Pierre Cuypers, although railroad engineer L. J. Eijmer was responsible for the two large, tubular platform concourses. The first train shed on the city side was completed in 1889, while the narrower and longer train shed facing the water, the IJ, was completed in 1922. The boarding platform areas between the two train sheds were covered in 1996. The station is actually built on three artificial islands, its stability guaranteed by countless wooden piles driven into the ground—recalling how Venice was built.
| Aerovista Luchtfotografe / Shutterstock

Groningen—the Netherlands

The railroad station in Groningen is a conventional through station. The station building faces the city, and it is equipped with long platforms along the eleven tracks for passenger service. This aerial photograph shows the train station—to the left of the station building, which some consider the most beautiful in the Netherlands—and the UWV building to the right (UWV: Uitvoeringsinstituut Werknemersverzekeringen, or Employee Insurance Agency). In the background is the Groninger Museum, which was built over the waters of the Zuiderhaven River. The photograph on the right shows the station building from the street side. Typical of late-nineteenth-century architecture, the facade displays a decorative mix of late Gothic and neo-Renaissance styles.
| Aerovista Luchtfotografe / Shutterstock + W. Bulach, CC BY-SA 4.0

Liège—Belgium

Liège-Guillemins station is the most important train station in Liège, in Belgium's Walloon region. The station sits just outside the city center, in the Guillemins district. The light-flooded structure was completed in September 2009 after extensive renovation and new construction. The old Liège-Guillemins station was outdated after the arrival of high-speed train service. In an international competition, the project was awarded to architect Santiago Calatrava, who had experience designing station architecture. The new station is built of steel, glass, and white concrete. It features a monumental canopy 200 m long and 35 m high. There are eleven station tracks with platforms up to 450 m long. This means that double multiple units of the French-Belgian rail operator Thalys can also stop here. | picture alliance / imageBROKERRoda

Strasbourg—France

Futuristic meets the historic at the Strasbourg-Ville station, the central train station in the capital city of the Grand Est region, which unites the former regions of Alsace, Champagne-Ardenne, and Lorraine. It was built on the site of the former Strasbourg Vauban fortifications. Construction began in 1878, inspired by a design by Berlin architect Johann Eduard Jacobsthal. Inaugurated on August 15, 1883, it replaced the old Strasbourg terminal station. However, construction wasn't completed until 1898. It is under special protection as a historical monument. As part of the process of connecting to the TGV (*train à grande vitesse*, or high-speed train) service, the station underwent significant reconstruction in 2006 and 2007. A glass wall in front of the station defined space for a new forecourt; the wall is vaulted at the top and connected to the building facade. An additional lower level was carved out under the forecourt. | picture alliance / imageBROKER

In France, many of the rail lines built during the 1900s had Paris as their main destination. Thus, it is hardly surprising that the French capital has six large terminal stations. Radial and tangential lines filled in the rail network; numerous branch lines serving the regions were closed in recent years. It was not until 1938 that the large number of big and small private railroad companies merged to form the SNCF (Société nationale des chemins de fer français—the French National Railroad), which not only promoted electrification but also built standardized infrastructure such as engine houses. The construction of the high-speed rail network for the TGV (train à grande vitesse, or high-speed train) was like a revolution: it started in 1981 with the newly built Paris–Lyon line, which was followed by many others. Individual TGV trains run only on conventional tracks in the railroad sections feeding into or branching from the high-speed network. To make medium-sized cities accessible, the choice has often been to build train stations a few kilometers away from the city center, and to locate them directly on the high-speed lines. Having the TGV trains stop at these stations is more efficient than if the trains had to leave the high-speed network to run on the old lines and then travel to the stations in the city center. While the first TGV stations were purely functional, the newer ones are considered architectural masterpieces.

Paris—France

With its splendid, landmark-protected decor dating from around 1900, the Le Train Bleu station restaurant at Gare de Lyon takes rail station dining to a new level. It was designed by Marius Toudoire, and the forty-one paintings inside the restaurant were commissioned from thirty painters. The murals depict the cities and regions that the PLM (Paris à Lyon et à la Méditerranée) rail network once connected to Paris. | picture alliance / imageBROKER

Paris—France

On the facade of the Gare du Nord, eight statues of women symbolize the important travel destinations: Brussels, Amsterdam, London, Vienna, Berlin, Warsaw, Cologne, and Frankfurt am Main. The station is in the Tenth Arrondissement, on Place Napoléon III, and is the most heavily traveled train station in Europe; worldwide, it is number three. Some 700,000 passengers pass through this terminal station every day. Its striking, neoclassical design dates to 1861, primarily the work of German architect Ignaz Hittorf, born in Cologne in 1792. At that time, France had annexed the Rhineland region, on the western bank of the Rhine River, and as a result, Hittorf had French citizenship. He moved to Paris in 1810. | picture alliance / image-BROKER

Europe 71

Paris—France

Bird's-eye view of Paris and the Montparnasse train station. The terminal station (one of six in Paris) was redesigned as part of a real estate project on the Place Raoul Dautry in 1990, when the first section of the LGV (*lignes à grande vitesse*, or high-speed rail line) Atlantique started operating. The station is especially busy during holidays because it is the departure point for the popular vacation regions in the west and southwest of France. A glass facade called Porte Océane offers a view of the concrete interior architecture and is intended to reinforce the idea of a train station. A parking lot was built under some sections of the tracks. The Jardin Atlantique, an approximately 150 by 230 m garden, lies on the roof, which spans twenty-two tracks. The old station, the scene of a spectacular railroad accident in 1895, shows up in one of the most famous photographs in railroad history: a locomotive derailed after its brakes failed, and burst through the wall of the station building, falling onto the street below.

| Kit Leong / Shutterstock

▲ **Paris—France**

A modern transportation station on different levels, linked together by escalators and elevators. This is how the light-flooded Montparnasse train station looks to travelers today. | picture alliance / imageBROKER

Paris—France

Only a daytime photograph can portray Montparnasse's extensive track system. This station serves the TGV Atlantique trains running west and southwest, among other train services. The station has twenty-eight aboveground tracks. TGV trains run on tracks 1 to 9 (*left*), Transilien commuter trains run on tracks 10 to 17, and the TER (Transport express régional) Centre and TGV trains run on tracks 18 to 24. There is a side wing, the Gare Vaugirard, where tracks 25 to 28 (*right*) are laid. From here, Corail Intercités (equivalent to German Intercity trains) and TER trains run east to the towns of Argentan and Granville.
| picture alliance / imageBROKER

▲ **Lyon—France**

The Gare de Lyon-Saint-Exupéry TGV station lies just outside this beautiful city on the Rhone River. First and foremost, it is a long-distance train station that connects Lyon Airport to the TGV network. Spanish star architect Santiago Calatrava designed the futuristic architecture. Other projects by Santiago Calatrava AG include the transfer station at Ground Zero in New York City, the Zurich Stadelhofestation, and the Liège-Guillemins station. The Lyon station is notable not only for its impressive architecture, but also for its huge cost overrun. Built at a cost of roughly six billion francs, the steel, glass, and reinforced-concrete building is 450 m long and 56 m wide, housing six tracks.

| picture alliance / Schütze/Rodemann / www.bildarch

Cerbère—France

Overview of the Cerbère train station in southern France, on the border with Spain. On the left you can see the roof of the station building as well as the train shed laid out along a curved track. Sidings are visible in the center, and the Mediterranean Sea greets us on the far right. The passenger station has three platforms along its five tracks, and the elongated station building is on the side facing away from the town. A special feature is the dead-end siding tracks alongside the station building platform. These tracks are laid in Spanish broad gauge; this is the terminal stop for trains coming from Barcelona via the Spanish border station of Portbou. The tracks to the left of the train station lead to a huge railroad yard laid out in fan pattern. It is used for handling freight and was literally dug into a mountain. | BOULENGER Xavier / Shutterstock

Angoulême—France

View of Angoulême train station in the Department of Charente in France. It is a junction station on the Paris–Bordeaux and the Limoges–Angoulême and Beillan–Angoulême rail lines. On the right is the station, originally built in 1852, with its train shed, which covers the four station tracks with platforms. A regional railcar sits to the left on the outer platform. While overhead catenary lines span the main tracks, this investment was not made for the freight tracks visible on the left. Instead, a diesel locomotive shunting is used there. | Leonid Andronov / Shutterstock

Madrid—Spain

The new Atocha train station in the Spanish capital city, Madrid, went into service in 1992. While regional train service is handled in an underground through station, the long-distance trains meet in a sunlit train shed, as shown in this photograph featuring several AVE (*alta velocidad española*, or Spanish high-speed) trains and Talgo articulated trains. However, the old art nouveau train shed has also been preserved, used as a waiting room and meeting point. Unfortunately, tragedy in March 2004 occurred when Islamist terrorists carried out a series of attacks in Madrid. There were seven explosions in the train station and its adjacent neighborhood. Nearly 200 fatalities were reported. A monument directly in front of the station commemorates those who lost their lives. | picture alliance / imageBROKER

On the Iberian Peninsula, trains traditionally run on broad-gauge tracks. In Portugal the state railroad, CP (Comboios de Portugal, or Trains of Portugal), also still operates a few narrow-gauge (1 meter [m] wide) lines, although most of these railroads were decommissioned in the 1980s. In Spain, European Union funding was also used to invest in the newly designed high-speed network: In 1992 the first high-speed line was built for AVE high-speed trains between Madrid and Seville. With foresight, this work was done in the European standard gauge. More routes were opened in the following years, with the French TGV serving as a model in terms of infrastructure and rolling stock. New railroad stations were built on the new routes, and thus the Madrid-Atocha station was replaced by a new building. Some existing broad-gauge lines have also been upgraded for the high-speed service; in most cases, these lines are extensions of the standard-gauge lines, so that "gauge-changing" trains will be used. In the last few decades, we have had to say farewell to many narrow-gauge railroads that were no longer able to cope with the competition from private transport.

Sóller—Spain

This aerial photograph dating from April 2020 shows the tracks and high-rise structures of the train station in Sóller on the holiday island of Mallorca. Service is handled by Ferrocarril de Sóller (Sóller Railways), which operates a branch line with 914 mm gauge to Palma, the capital of Mallorca, and a streetcar line to the port of Sóller. The small rail yard, with turntable and roundhouse, is clearly visible in the right half of the picture.
| picture alliance / ZB / euroluftbild.de

Madrid—Spain

The Atocha train station is one of two long-distance train stations in Madrid; the track "throat" area for the switches and crossings is shown here. Service began at the new station in 1992. Since then, the old station train shed, featuring a palm garden, has served as a meeting point for the Madrilenians. Today's train station is built in two sections. The long-distance trains, including the AVE high-speed train to Seville, end in the aboveground part of the station, which has once again been built as a terminus. Regional trains and urban rapid-transit trains use an underground through station that is connected to three double-track tunnels. | Leonid Andronov / Shutterstock

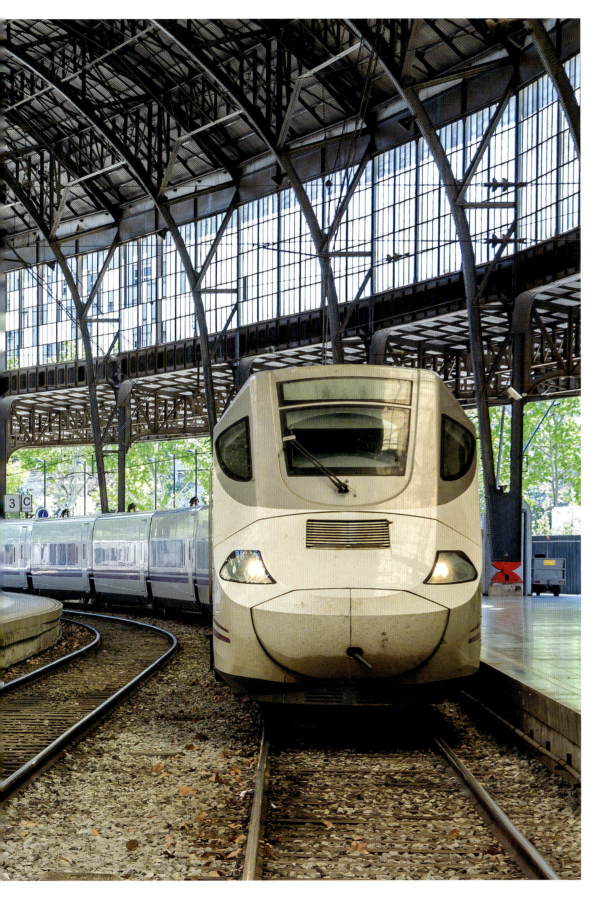

Barcelona—Spain

Estació de França (Catalan for the Train Station of France) is a long-distance and regional train station in the Catalan metropolis of Barcelona. It is the second most important in the city after the Barcelona-Sants train station. This terminal station was built in its current form for the Barcelona International Exposition in 1929. The 29 m high and 195 m long train shed is impressive with its two vaults. One section of the tracks in the shed is curved.

| Alberto Zampano / Shutterstock

Europe **85**

Porto—Portugal

Not much was going on when this photograph was taken at the São Bento train station in May 2017. The first trains ran to São Bento in 1896. However, the station building went into service in 1916. The station is built on the site of the former Mosteiro de São Bento de Avé-Maria monastery; today only the name of the monastery remains. Because this through station is located in the inner city, it was also necessary to dig three tunnels, one of which lies directly at the station exit. The station has been electrified since 1966. So far, its historic-landmark status (since 1997) has protected it from a proposal to replace it with a shopping center. | Mirjam Claus / Shutterstock

Lisbon—Portugal

The Gare do Oriente (East Station) was built in time for the 1998 Lisbon World Exposition. Architect Santiago Calatrava won the 1994 design competition, and construction began a year later. Designed as a through station for long-distance, regional, and local train service, the tracks are 14 m above street level and spanned by a delicate glass-roof structure. The building's blend of the natural and high-tech is typical of the architect. For example, the refined glass roof resembles ribbed leaves. Stairs, escalators, and elevators lead from the platforms to the concourse with the ticket counters and kiosks. | monterio.online/ Shutterstock

Aveiro—Portugal

Colorful works of art made of ornamental tiles, called *azulejos*, decorate many Portuguese train stations. This includes the old station building in the city of Aveiro, which is now used for art exhibitions. *Azulejos* form a picture out of mostly square, colorfully painted and glazed ceramic tiles. In Europe, this art form originated in Spain and Portugal. The weatherproof tiles are an integral part of the cityscape in these countries. The *azulejos* in this photograph show the station building, among other images. | Marina J. / Shutterstock

Bolzano—Italy

This view of the train station of Bolzano (or Bozen in German, the language spoken by most people in the Italian province of South Tyrol) is from Renon, or Ritten Mountain. Bolzano has a junction station that connects the Brenner Railway and the Bolzano–Merano (Meran) railroad line. International Eurocity long-distance trains that connect Germany, Austria, and Italy stop here. Travelers can find a fast connection to Rome via the Frecciargento high-speed trains. The Bolzano train station is of great importance as a full-scale hub in the regional fixed-interval train timetable. Local rail transport is provided by Trenitalia trains, as does the SAD (Società Automobilistica Dolomiti, or Dolomite Bus Service), which operates bus services to the station along with the SASA (Società Autobus Servizi d'Area, or Municipal Bus Service). Designed by Austrian engineer Alois Negrelli, the rail station opened in 1859. During the Fascist period in Italy, Angiolo Mazzoni oversaw the redesign of the station building, which opened for service in 1928 (*visible to the right of the tracks*). The building suffered severe damage during World War II but was quickly repaired. In the first decade of the 2000s, Centostazioni, the train station operator, rebuilt it. Incidentally, the Bolzano train station wasn't Alois Negrelli's only railroad project. Among other commissions, he was project manager of the first railroad built entirely on Swiss soil, the Swiss Northern Railway, between Baden in Aargau and Zurich (it was nicknamed the Spanish-Brötli railroad after a pastry for which Baden was famous). Many other railroad lines were built in Austria under his leadership. Among them was the Vienna–Prague rail line, which was completed in two stages. Thus, Negrelli was a railroad pioneer. This industrious civil engineer also played a decisive role in the Suez Canal design: he is credited for the plan to build the canal without locks.

| picture alliance / imageBROKER

The history of the railroad in Italy began in 1839, when the first railroad began operating on the peninsula between Naples and Portici, a town just to the south. A state-owned railroad was formed after the unification of the greatest part of the private and state-owned railroads in 1905; it has been operating most of the rail service in Italy ever since. Italian trains run on standard-gauge tracks, while there are also numerous branch lines that are laid in a narrow gauge of 950 mm. Since Italy does not have its own coal reserves, electrification began as early as 1900. Nevertheless, the steam engine was able to hold its own until the 1980s, several years longer than in other central European countries. Italy also has an important locomotive industry, including the Ansaldo, Breda, and Fiat companies, which are successful exporters. The construction of high-speed lines began around forty years ago, and some have replaced existing lines. Thus, as a contrast, you can find magnificent old station buildings in big cities, dreamy and partly empty country stations, and new transport stations where renowned designers were allowed to "let off steam."

Genoa—Italy

Genova Piazza Principe train station is one of the two main stations in the Italian port city of Genoa. It is located in the northwest area of the city center, between Piazza Acquaverde and Piazza del Principe. The station building (*far left*) takes up the entire northern section of the Via Andrea Doria. Service facilities are at street level, while the track systems and platform are one level lower. The station was built in 1860 under the direction of architect Alessandro Mazzucchetti. Back then, a steel train shed spanned the tracks in a wide arc. Today, wide platform canopies protect passengers from inclement weather. Our gaze is directed to the west. If you were to turn around, you would be looking at large tunnel portals: the tracks disappear into a tunnel, which allows it to pass under large parts of the city center. The tunnel ends at Genova Brignole station.
| StockphotoVideo / Shutterstock

Manarola—Italy

Tourists wait for the train on a platform in Manarola, in the Cinque Terre area of Italy. Manarola, on the Liguria coast, has a railroad station on the Pisa–Genoa rail line, which connects it with La Spezia and Sestri Levante. The train station sits by the sea and is connected to the village via a 100 m long tunnel. The station tracks follow the coastline in a slight curve, then they disappear into tunnels in both directions. Many tunnels were to built to traverse the rocky coastline.
| picture alliance / Rolf Haid

Reggio Emilia—Italy

Reggio Emilia AV (*alta velocità*, or high speed) Mediopadana railroad station is the only stop for high-speed trains on the Milan–Bologna section of the line and opened for passengers in June 2013. The train station, designed by the Spanish architect Santiago Calatrava, whom we encounter again and again in this book, is considered a masterpiece of modern architecture. Its cavernous station concourse is 483 m long, 35 to 50 m wide, and an average of 20 m high. The white-steel-and-glass structure, undulating horizontally and vertically, resembles a sequence of waves. The photograph shows a section of the side "wall."
| picture alliance / imageBROKER

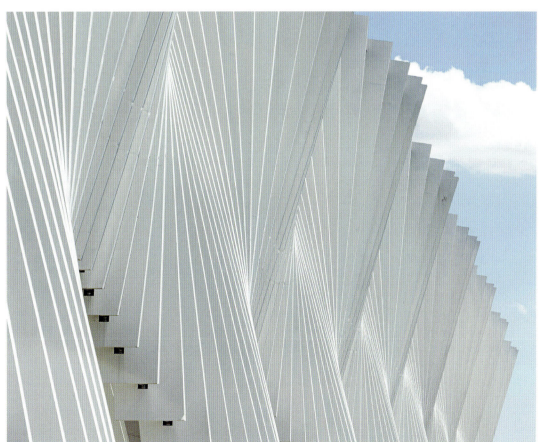

Venice—Italy

This aerial photograph shows Venice and the Santa Lucia Central Station—a terminus and the only train station on the island of Venice. It takes its name from the church of Santa Lucia that originally stood on this site and was demolished to make way for the station in 1861. A memorial stone in the middle of the square commemorates the former church. The railroad station's current appearance is the result of a series of designs created since 1924 by architects Angiolo Mazzoni and Virgilio Vallot (1901–1982), who won a design competition in 1934. The architects worked together on the station building and train shed from 1936 to 1943. Construction continued after the end of World War II under the direction of architect Paolo Perilli and was completed in 1952. The station is connected to the Venezia Mestre junction station on the mainland (*pictured above*) via the Ponte della Libertà (Bridge of Freedom) and thus to the rest of the FS (Ferrovie dello Stato Italiane, or Italian State Railroad) network. Incidentally, in front of the station there are no streetcars, buses, or cabs awaiting the traveler to Venice; instead, eight vaporetto (water bus) lines serve various destinations along Venice's canals.
| Aerial-motion/Shutterstock

Europe 93

Turin—Italy

Torino Porta Susa is a long-distance and regional train station in the Italian city of Turin and is now the city's most important train station. The first two tracks of this tunnel station opened in 2008; when the old aboveground station was finally closed, two more tracks were opened in the station, actually called Torino Porta Susa sotterranea (underground). The station was moved after a decision to banish the railroad underground for urban-planning reasons. Thus, Porta Susa replaced Porta Nuova as Turin's main station. The tunnel station is covered by a steel-and-glass structure 300 m long and 19 m high. | picture alliance / robertharding

Rome—Italy

Roma Tiburtina, a through station, is the second-largest train station in Rome after Roma Termini. Located in the northeastern part of the Italy's capital city, it has an impressive twenty station tracks with platforms. Its origins go back to 1866. Time and again it has been expanded and modernized. The new station building, inaugurated in 2011, runs at an elevated diagonal and spans the entire system of tracks. The building is around 300 m long and sits about 9 m above the tracks. The bridge concourse also links the city districts of Nomentano and Pietralata, which were previously separated by the railroad line. Inside are ticket counters, waiting rooms, shops, and other facilities for travelers, some of which are suspended like berths halfway up the height of the concourse. The outer facade is clad with glass. | picture alliance / dpa

Lanusei—Italy

The Lanusei train station runs on the Sardinian narrow-gauge railroad (950 mm) between the towns of Mandas and Arbatax. Today it is used primarily by tourists, and the Trenino Verde (small green trains) passenger service runs only in summer. However, the rail service is currently suspended for technical reasons. The typical country station, 554 m above sea level, once served rush-hour traffic of the 5,000-person municipality, especially in the direction of Arbatax. The elegant railcar is one of the ADe series.
| picture alliance / imageBROKER

Palermo—Italy

The Stazione di Palermo Centrale provides the Sicilian capital city with a magnificent terminal train station. Opened in 1886, the station building has a neoclassical flair, a reminder of the many architectural gems that this lively city has to offer. Despite the destruction it suffered during World War II, Palermo, overshadowed for so long by the scourge of the Mafia, features architecture from diverse periods and styles. Five canopied platforms accommodate passengers along the ten tracks for arrivals and departures. The station is operated by the state-owned Rete Ferroviaria Italiana (Italian Railroad Network) and is the starting point of the Palermo–Agrigent / Porto Empedocle line and the Palermo–Trapani line. It is also an important transport hub for the suburban rail network, the Servizio ferroviario metro politano di Palermo (Palermo Metropolitan Train Service). | picture alliance / ZB / euroluftbild.de

Kalamata—Greece

The once-extensive meter-gauge rail network on the Peloponnese Peninsula in Greece has been largely decommissioned, although some sections are being switched to standard gauge. The former terminals station at Kalamata (the last train ran in 2010) is now used as a railroad park, which displays vehicles from railroading history. The photograph shows, among other things, a steam locomotive and tender (coal car) with two-axle passenger cars and a fast railcar reminiscent of the German SVT (Schnellverkehrs-Triebwagen, rapid-transit railcar), which once traveled at a brisk pace through the Peleponnes region. | Pit Stock / Shutterstock

Olympia—Greece

The ruins of ancient Olympia lie in a plain at the foot of Mount Kronos on the bank of the river Kladeos, shortly before its confluence with the Alfos on the Peloponnese Peninsula. Olympia station, with its slightly antique look, is the terminus of a 33 km rail line from Katakolon, a popular stopover for cruise ships. So it is primarily cruise ship passengers who travel on the meter-gauge railcar to Olympia. | picture alliance / ASA

The first train in Greece ran between Athens and Piraeus in 1869. Primarily serving urban local transport, this connection still exists as part of the Athens subway network. In contrast to other European countries, railroads play only a niche role in Greece. Only the main route from Idomeni via Tessaloniki to Athens has any significance. For many years, many of the German trains with their own names, such as the Hellas Express from Dortmund or the Acropolis Express from Munich, rolled along this line.

In the meantime, this main line has been expanded to two tracks and electrified, but travelers from central Europe have long preferred to fly. A true railroad network existed only on the Peleponnes Peninsula, where the many meter-gauge lines made the countryside quite accessible—even offering long-distance trains with sleeping and dining cars. Today this network has largely been shut down or the gauge is being changed to standard gauge, thanks to European Union funding. The end of the Greek state railroad OSE (Hellenic Railways Organisation) came in 2017, when the railroad network was sold to FS Italia, and only the rolling stock remained in Greek hands. Modernization in recent years has resulted in the construction of many new transport stations; functionality is their primary characteristic.

Europe **99**

II. AFRICA—CONTINENT OF CONTRASTS

The railroads in the Maghreb countries of Algeria, Morocco, and Tunisia are still strongly influenced by those of France, the former colonial power, although the three countries achieved their independence more than fifty years ago. In contrast to South Africa, for example, the Maghreb railroads run mostly on standard-gauge tracks, apart from the extensive narrow-gauge (1 m wide) network in southern Tunisia. Some of the rolling stock comes from France, such as the Moroccan TGV trains, but also from the United States and Canada. Passenger service is largely in modern, air-conditioned cars; freight trains are used to transport mineral resources. The railroads in Egypt can also look back on a long history: the line between Cairo and Alexandria started service between 1854 and 1865 as the first railroad line in the Middle East and Africa; it was planned and built by the famous Robert Stephenson from England. Even today, some parts of the railroad infrastructure in Egypt have the appearance of being "quite British"—no wonder, since the country was under British rule from 1882 to 1922, until it gained full sovereignty in 1936. In 2005, the seminational railroad organization Egypt National Railways (ENR) operated a total of 5,063 km of rail lines in European standard gauge. The greater part of the network connects the densely populated area of the Nile delta with the urban centers of Cairo and Alexandria. The Alexandria–Cairo–Luxor–Aswan connection is a daily service with air-conditioned sleeper trains operated by the private company Abela. These trains are intended for tourists. There is also a comfortable express train that connects the Ramses train station in Cairo with Marsa Matruh (near the Libyan border). Around 2025, a new high-speed line from Alexandria to Aswan is due to start running. All the railroads in North Africa said goodbye to the last steam locomotives more than fifty years ago, replacing them with diesel and electric locomotives as well as railcar trains.

Marrakesh—Morocco

Morocco has a relatively modern railroad system, yet the influence of France, the former colonial power, is still clearly visible. Since 1963, the ONCF (Office National des Chemins de Fer) has operated the national rail service. The backbone of the rail network, which has 2,110 km of track and 133 stations, is the line from Oujda on the Algerian border, via Fez and Casablanca, to Marrakesh, where several terminal branch lines diverge. Almost 1,600 km of the routes have been electrified, and further expansion work is under construction or in the planning stage. This photograph gives us a view over the new train station in Marrakesh with arriving passengers. It was built in 2008 in the immediate vicinity of the old station, dating from 1923. | picture alliance / dpa

101

Algiers—Algeria

Rail transport in Algeria was founded by a large number of private railroad companies and was largely nationalized during the French colonial rule. Today the railroads are operated as a national system, and a streetcar and a subway network are being built in Algiers. The Algiers railroad station lies just a street away from the port. The station is shown here on March 25, 2019, along with a modern electric multiple-unit train, a Stadler Flirt, which has been in service in the Algiers urban rapid-transit network since 2009. The station building dates back to colonial times, and the same is true of the large train shed. | picture alliance / Johannes Glöckner

Oran—Algeria

The train station building in the Algerian city of Oran, built by the French during colonial times, is kept in an orientalist (Moorish revival) architectural style. The architect, who also designed the Sacré Cœur Cathedral in Oran, was the Frenchman Albert Ballu, who died in 1939. From a structural point of view, it is interesting that reinforced concrete, a modern material, was used in both buildings, despite the historicized appearance. The Oran terminus is the final stop on a terminal branch line that connects to the main Algiers–Sidi bel Abbes line at Qued. | picture alliance / robertharding

El Alamein—Egypt

Exterior view of the train station in El Alamein, taken on January 10, 2014. This old, dilapidated railroad station on the Alexandria–Marsa Matruh line became famous because, shortly after the two World War II battles between Allied troops and units of the Axis powers near El Alamein, British reburial detachments moved the fallen of both sides to a temporary resting place near the station. A new line from El Alamein to Ain Sukhna is being considered. | Matthias Tödt / picture alliance / ZB

Alexandria—Egypt

Hustle and bustle in front of the main railroad station in the Egyptian metropolis with five million inhabitants, Alexandria. A largely glazed train shed is connected to the magnificent station building of the terminus. Egyptian National Railways represents the backbone of passenger transport in Egypt and provides service for around 800 million passengers annually. Air-conditioned trains usually offer both first- and second-class service. Second and third class are the usual services offered on non-air-conditioned trains. The Alexandria–Cairo–Luxor–Aswan connection is a daily service with air-conditioned sleeper trains operated by the private Abela company. These trains are specially designed for tourists. | picture alliance /Herve Champollion / akg-images

Nouadhibou—Mauritania

The Nouadhibou–M'Haoudat railroad is the only railroad line in Mauritania. It connects the iron ore mines near the interior town of Zouérat with the port city of Nouadhibou on the Atlantic coast. The route, initially 652 km long, was built in standard gauge starting in 1957 by the operator of the iron ore mines at the time, the Société Anonyme des Mines de fer de la Mauritanie (Mauritanian Iron Mines Company). The line runs between the Atlantic port of Nouadhibou and the ore mines at Choum and Zouérat and started service in June 1963. Later, a terminal branch line around 70 km long was added, running to the M'Haoudat mine—which branches off from the station at the town of F'dérik. The long ore trains, some of which are hauled by up to five heavy diesel locomotives, at times also include secondhand passenger railroad cars brought over from Europe. You can board them at train stations that don't have a building, such as shown here at the Zouérate terminus. Since 1999 there has been a modest tourist service, run under the name Train du désert, that offers a sleeping car and a double-decker car.

| picture alliance / Godong

The decade-long decline of railroads in East Africa is coming to an end. Many routes have been shut down or have suspended passenger service forever, but investment from China is contributing to a railroad renaissance. In Ethiopia and Tanzania, for example, new lines make comfortable and, above all, relatively fast travel possible with their modern rolling stock—which also, of course, comes from the People's Republic of China. In Kenya, too, there are signs of a railroad comeback. Here, the future lies on standard-gauge (1,435 mm) tracks—the classic Cape gauge (1,076 mm) has almost had its day. In Mauritania, trains still run on Cape-gauge tracks to a large extent, but an ore railroad more than 700 km long, which runs on standard gauge, deserves mention. On this railroad, freight trains weighing up to 10,000 tons are powered by six-axle EMD (Electro-Motive Diesel) locomotives from the United States in a multitraction system. Incidentally, there are no train stations here, although the population is allowed to ride on the freight cars free of charge.

Addis Ababa—Ethiopia

The new Addis Ababa train station on August 10, 2017, with a Chinese-built passenger train. The standard-gauge line, which opened in 2016, connects the Ethiopian capital city of Addis Ababa to the port city of Djibouti. It was built with financial support from China and runs at speeds of up to 160 km per hour. Sections of the line run parallel to the abandoned narrow, meter-gauge line, built between 1894 and 1917. It runs on a new train path, does not use any of the infrastructure of the historical line, and is almost 30 km shorter than the other one was. The Addis Ababa Lebu station was built as the main station in Addis Ababa to accommodate passenger service. It lies southwest of the city center in a suburb of the same name. The design of the three-story station building, completed in September 2015, references the cultural heritage of the Oromo people.
| picture alliance / Johannes Glöckner

Mombasa—Kenya

The new Mombasa Terminus station, here photographed on August 11, 2017, looks like an airport terminal. The China-built, 472 km, standard-gauge line to Nairobi opened in May 2017. Two diesel locomotives and generator cars power the fully air-conditioned cars, which were also built in China. Passenger trains run twice a day in both directions as the Madaraka Express, with an intermediate stop at the train junction at the town of Mtito Andei. Seats are available in first- and second-class cars. The express trains initially offered around 1,200 seats, but a few weeks later they accommodated 1,500 passengers. | picture alliance / Johannes Glöckner

Moshi—Tanzania

In January 2017, a lonely freight car served as a reminder of the railroad traffic at the Moshi railroad station in Tanzania, formerly German East Africa. A railroad company founded in 1891 connected the port of Tanga on the Indian Ocean to Lake Victoria on a route running along the foothills of the Usambara Mountains. Construction of the Usambara Railway began two years later, and in 1911 the meter-wide, narrow-gauge track reached Moshi. After World War I, the British Mandate administration extended the railway by building a link between Moshi and the town of Voi in Kenya, on the Uganda Line of the Kenya and Uganda Railway. They extended it to its present terminus at Arusha in 1929. | Sergey-73/Shutterstock

Moshi—Tanzania

Railroad facilities at Moshi, shown in 2017 after the temporary suspension of all rail service. Following a directive from President Magufuli, work began on rehabilitating the line in June 2018. In October 2018, it was possible to run a rail service between the port of Tanga and interior town of Mombo once again. On July 20, 2019, Prime Minister Kassim Majaliwa reopened freight traffic between Tanga and Moshi. The first train was an 800-ton cement train. Cement transport is cheaper and more reliable by railroad, given the poor roads. The first continuous passenger train from Dar es Salaam to Moshi ran on December 7, 2019. Plans are being made for the resumption of traffic to Arusha. | Sergey-73/Shutterstock

The nations of West Africa also intend to give railroads a bigger share of transport once again. This is true for the countries of the West African Economic and Monetary Union (WAEMU)—Benin, Burkina Faso, Ivory Coast, Mali, Niger, Senegal, Togo, and Guinea-Bissau—and the countries of the G5 Sahel zone—Mauritania, Mali, Niger, Burkina Faso, and Chad—as well as Nigeria. Here, too, Chinese investment will carry this out; China announced in 2015 that it would make up to $600 billion available for an efficient rail network. The West African countries consider two railroad projects to be the most urgent: the Abidjan–Ouagadougou–Niamey–Cotonou railroad loop and the Trans-Sahel Railroad, connecting Nouakchott, Bamako, Ouagadougou, Niamey, and N'Djamena.

Dimbokro—Ivory Coast

This railroad station of the Sitarail railroad company is on the international line between the Ivory Coast port city of Abidjan and Ouagadougou, Burkina Faso. The station has a modern station building with a waiting hall with ticket counter and baggage handling. It has three station tracks with platforms and one track that is used only by freight traffic. Passenger trains also use the station. The trains to Ouagadougou, Burkina Faso, stop here three times a week (Tuesday, Thursday, Saturday), and the return trains to Abidjan also stop three times a week (Monday, Wednesday, Friday). The trains offer first- and second-class passenger cars. Some of them have express service with fewer intermediate stops. | Gregor Rom, CC BY-SA 4.0

Beira—Mozambique

The station building of Beira train station in Mozambique, built in 1966, exudes 1960s charm. The railroad network around Beira, built in Cape gauge, has been modernized in recent years. Nevertheless, passenger service remains sparse: once a week, a pair of trains run between Beira and Marromeu, and another pair of trains run between Beira and Moatize. The station building has two parts—the office building and the entrance hall to the railroad station. A large, arched roof with seven struts spans the single-story, 57 m high train shed, and ten double-door entrances allow access to the station. The seven-story office building, with its striking vertical elements that offer shade, towers above the roofed train shed. The design, by three architects, is modern and functional. | picture alliance / africamediaonline

Southern African countries, such as Namibia, Zimbabwe, and South Africa itself, can look back on a long tradition of railroading, mainly due to the activities of the former colonial powers. In South Africa, the railroad era began in Durban as early as 1860. Today the network is around 20,000 km long, with roughly 95 percent of it in the typical Cape gauge—an English invention, with the internal spacing between the two rail heads amounting to 3.5 English feet. Today, the railroad is particularly important for freight transport. In addition, there is an efficient local transport network in South Africa, most of which is electrified and, in individual cases, built in standard gauge. For a long time, South Africa was considered a paradise for steam locomotives, a fact that is recalled by the many steam engines there, some of which are kept in working order and used at the front of special trains. There are also luxury trains designed for tourists, such as the Blue Train and the Pride of Africa. The longest route, along which the Pride of Africa—considered the most luxurious train in the world—runs, is from Cape Town, South Africa, to Dar es Salaam, Tanzania.

Maputo—Mozambique

The train station of Maputo, in Portuguese usually called the Estação do Caminho de Ferro de Maputo (Maputo Railway) or CFM for short, is the main train station of the capital city of Mozambique. It is located on Praça dos Trabalhadores in the Baixa district. The terminal station building was built between 1908 and 1910 according to plans by architects Alfredo Augusto Lisboa de Lima, Mário Veiga, and Ferreira da Costa. CFM, the national railroad company, operates the daily passenger train service. However, there is only a single train service operating on the three lines served (Linha de Goba, Linha de Ressano Garcia, and Linha de Limpopo), and no regular timetable. The most-frequent train connections run to the two suburbs: Matola and Marracuene. | picture alliance / Design Pics

Garub—Namibia

Garub is an oasis, an abandoned railroad station, and a ghost town in the Karas region of southern Namibia. The small town of Garub was founded by the German Schutztruppe (the Protection Forces, the German colonial troops in Africa during the German imperial period, late nineteenth century until the end of World War I), who manned the station of the same name. It lies between Lüderitz and Aus on the railroad line between coastal Lüderitz and Seeheim. Garub in turn bore the name of the abundant springs in the Namib coastal desert, which were used to replenish the water supplies of steam locomotives. In contrast to the existing 600 mm, narrow-gauge network of tracks in the northern part of what then was German Southwest Africa, the gauge used for the Lüderitz–Garub–Aus line was the same as that of neighboring South Africa; namely, the 1,067 mm Cape gauge. The Deutsche Kolonial-Eisenbahn-Bau- und Betriebsgesellschaft (DKEBBG) (German Colonial Railroad Construction and Operating Company) built and operated the railroad. Construction began at the end of 1905, and trains started running to Aus as early as November 1, 1906. The construction company laid the subgrade, while the Schutztruppe railroad battalion built the surface track system. After a period without service, the Lüderitz Railway, it was rebuilt between 2001 and 2014. However, drifting sand made it impossible to schedule train service. Regular use resumed in 2019 after a section of the tracks was relocated to run through a tunnel, protected from the sand. The elevated steel water tanks where steam locomotives once quenched their thirst can be seen in the background, to the right of the tracks. | Nick Fox / Shutterstock

Bloemfontein—South Africa

View of the Bloemfontein Railway Station in South Africa with Bophelo House in the background. Bophelo House is the headquarters for the Department of Health and other government offices of the Free State, a province of South Africa. Bloemfontein is a railroad hub in the Free State and has a large through station with wide canopied platforms. The entryways to the platforms, built like bridges, are also clearly visible. A railroad linking the city to Cape Town has been around since 1890. Another railroad line runs north to Johannesburg. Only freight trains run on the route to Bethlehem. | picture alliance / ZB / euroluftbild.de

Johannesburg—South Africa

Passenger car sidings for the Metrorail Gauteng commuter rail service are pictured against the Johannesburg skyline. This company operates most of the local rail transport. Metrorail Gauteng local trains offer connections to Carletonville, Randfontein, and Soweto to the west, and Springs, Nigel, and Daveyton to the east. Pretoria is the system's northern destination, and to the south is a connection to Vereeniging.
| picture alliance / imageBROKER

Muizenberg—South Africa

The railroad station in Muizenberg, a coastal town in the South African province of Western Cape, is an architectural gem. The neoclassical building is the most elaborate along the entire railroad line, and a stellar example of the Edward VII era. On October 2, 1981, the South African Heritage Resources Agency declared it a protected historic landmark. The station lies on the electrically operated Southern Line (also called the Simon's Town Line), which connects Cape Town with Simon's Town. Passenger trains offer service to the tourist attractions south of Cape Town, such as Muizenberg, Kalk Bay, Fish Hoek, and Simon's Town. From Muizenberg, the route runs along the coast of False Bay.
| picture alliance / imageBROKER

Africa **121**

Pretoria—South Africa

Rovos Rail is the rail division of South Africa's Rovos Rail Tours Ltd., which runs a luxury train service on the narrow Cape-gauge network in southern Africa. Its "home station" is the former Capital Park Station rail yard, north of Pretoria. Capital Park Station was once a railroad junction; its brick art deco train station has been lovingly restored and complements the Rovos Rail trains. In addition to around sixty railroad cars, the company owns four steam locomotives. Rohan Ross founded Rovos Rail in 1989. Its various routes operate on an annual schedule in South Africa and beyond. The trains are made up of historical South African passenger coaches that have been converted and luxuriously refurbished to offer the highest level of comfort. | Africanstar/Shutterstock

Durban—South Africa

Durban, formerly Port Natal, is a large city on the Indian Ocean, on the east coast of South Africa. This aerial photograph shows the city in the background; in front rises the 56,000-seat Moses Mabhida Stadium, built for the FIFA World Cup in 2010. With its striking central arch, it is a new landmark of the coastal region. To its right lies the extensive track system of the main Durban Railway Station. Transnet provides the long-distance transport, while Metrorail Durban operates the extensive suburban network. | Shutterstock/michaeljung

Manakara—Madagascar

Manakara station, preserved in the old French colonial style, lies at the end of a 162 km long, narrow-gauge line from the city of Fianarantsoa. On April 14, 2019, a passenger train pulled by a diesel locomotive halts in the golden morning light as travelers board the train and the last of their luggage is loaded aboard. The passengers have an interesting journey ahead; they will cross not only sixty-seven bridges, but also an airport runway!
| Frank Herben / Shutterstock

III. ASIA AND THE MIDDLE EAST— GREAT DIVERSITY

TCDD (Taşımacılık), the Turkish State Railways company, emerged from the nationalization of private railroad companies in the Republic of Turkey between the years 1921 and 1953. The railroad era in what is now Turkey began in 1860 in the Aegean coastal city of Izmir, with the construction of a rail line to Aydin. In the years that followed, the standard-gauge network was constantly expanded and the large cities were connected by rail. This expansion continued until 1950; meanwhile, however, even up to the present, service is often limited to only one daily pair of trains, especially on branch lines. The construction of the Marmaray Tunnel in 2013 made it possible to connect the TCDD network in European Turkey to the rail lines on Turkey's Anatolia peninsula (the westernmost region of the Asian continent)—thus the Turkish railroads now connect the continents of Europe and Asia. Thanks to the construction of high-speed lines, the railroads in Turkey have become more important than they were at the turn of the millennium.

Istanbul—Turkey

Drone photograph from 2016 showing Istanbul's Haydarpaşa railroad station and its immediate neighborhood. This terminal rail station is on the Asian side of the Bosporus Strait, within the Haydarpaşa harbor area. The combined freight and port railroad station is north of the passenger station. The German construction company Philipp Holzmann built the Haydarpasa station, and German architects Otto von Kühlmann (a hereditary knight) and Hellmuth Cuno drew the plans. Construction began on May 30, 1906. Otto Linnemann, from Frankfurt am Main, designed the windows in the station concourse. Opening on August 19, 1908, it was the starting point for the historic Anatolian Railway; the Baghdad Railway line branched off to the east. The Turkish railroad lines to Anatolia, Iran, Iraq, and Syria started at Haydarpaşa station. Beginning in 1930, it was also the starting point for the Taurus Express. In February 2012, long-distance service to Haydarpaşa station was suspended. As part of the Marmaray project, which built a tunnel under the Bosporus, after 2014 the station was no longer the terminus of the urban rapid-transit trains running on the Anatolian Railway to Istanbul's eastern suburbs. However, long-distance service has resumed, and plans to convert it into a shopping center are off the table.
| Sahan Nuhoglu / Shutterstock

Istanbul—Turkey

Istanbul Sirkeci is a train station of the Turkish State Railways (TCDD) line in Sirkeci, a district in the European part of Istanbul. International, domestic, and regional trains run westward from here. This terminal station became famous as the final destination of the Orient Express. The terminus, originally known as the Müşir–Ahmet-Paşa station, opened on November 3, 1890, replacing the temporary station dating from 1873. The architect was August Jasmund, a Prussian construction official sent by the German government to Istanbul to study Ottoman architecture. This station complex, on a 1,200 m² site, is one of the greatest examples of European orientalist style and influenced the work of other architects. At the time, it was considered extremely modern because of its gas lighting and its heating system. The building has largely been preserved in its original condition. As part of the Marmaray project, the railroad tunnel between Europe and Asia, a subway station was built under the existing train station in 2013. | Lepneva Irina / Shutterstock

Israel Railways was created in 1948 out of sections of the standard-gauge Palestine Railways (PR) in Israel, the Haifa–Beirut–Tripoli (HBT) railroad line. It was built by the British military with US assistance during World War II, incorporating remnants of the narrow-gauge Hejaz Railway that remained in Israel. Yet, because of the routes these rail lines follow, which only partially corresponded to the settlement structure of the new state of Israel, the railroad played only a minor role in Israel for a long time. Since the end of the 1990s, however, the rail network has been considerably expanded and extended, especially the passenger service. Today more than 200 double-decker railcars are in use in Israel. The railcars were built in the Bombardier Transportation plant in Görlitz, eastern Germany, and run behind modern diesel locomotives.

Tel Aviv—Israel

Israel's modern railroad system is heavily influenced by German rolling stock. This photograph from March 2019 shows a local train entering Tel Aviv's Central Railroad Station. The train is made up of red double-decker railcars that are almost identical to those run by Germany's Deutsche Bahn AG. It is pulled by a Vossloh Euro 4000 diesel locomotive with fleet number 1401. The Israeli railroad network has expanded significantly in the last thirty years, and the fleet of rolling stock has been renewed.

| Yoav Tabakman / Shutterstock

Asia and the Middle East 129

Tel Aviv—Israel

The old Tel Aviv railroad station complex, on the historical railroad line between Jaffa and Jerusalem, has been given a new lease on life in a phase of restoration that lasted more than five years. However, this was not to restore the station to its original purpose, but rather to become a spacious cultural and leisure space within the commuting area of Israel's Mediterranean metropolis. In 1900, Hugo Wieland, a templar from Germany, settled near the train station and built a factory to produce roof tiles and bricks. His proximity to the station allowed him to transport his heavy products to the port of Jaffa at low cost and then ship them all over the world. The buildings where the bricks and tiles were produced, the loading train station, the Villa Wieland, and the impressive 1880 station building are now part of the beautiful grounds. | Boyan Georgiev / Shutterstock

Shiraz—Iran

The Shiraz Railroad Station is important for tourism and has been expanded accordingly. Shiraz, population 1.6 million, is in southern Iran. This terminal station, whose station building is considered the largest in the country, is the final destination on the Badrud–Isfahan–Shiraz railroad line. The rail line is operated by Railways of the Islamic Republic of Iran (RAI). | Uskarp/Shutterstock

Shiraz—Iran

A look into the concourse of the main train station in Tehran, the Iranian capital city, shows the arrival and departure display system as well as propaganda for the country's current rulers. The station was built in 1928–29 as part of the construction of the Trans-Iranian Railway and opened in 1930. In 1935, the German Philipp Holzmann AG company and its Swiss subsidiary, Softec, won the contract to construct the Tehran railroad station, in particular the station building, from the Danish company Kampsax, general contractor of the Trans-Iranian Railway. The station building and the adjoining building were the first reinforced-concrete structures erected in Iran. The skeleton was clad in different-colored travertine and polished limestone slabs. The station building was designed in the neoclassical style, which has often been used for public buildings around the world. | Janos Rautonen / Shutterstock

Rail transport in Iran is operated primarily by the RAI rail company, which stands for Railways of the Islamic Republic of Iran. Beyond this, some private railroad companies and local companies offer local public transport. The railroads in Iran are part of the European standard-gauge network and apply its norms. In the region close to the border with Iran's northern neighbors, short lines have been built in Russian broad gauge, making it possible to connect to the networks in Armenia, Azerbaijan, and Turkmenistan. The gauge-changing facilities for converting the rolling stock to the broad gauge are in the Iranian border stations. The plan was to expand Iran's rail network to a length of 25,000 km by 2025, but this seems unlikely because of the almost global economic sanctions against the country. Thus, the construction and delivery of Eurorunner diesel locomotives from the German Siemens company were largely handled "silently." The figures demonstrate that the railroad expansion is worthwhile when compared to road transport: between 2013 and 2017, the share of rail in the total transport volume rose from 4.4 to 12.8 percent.

Asia and the Middle East **131**

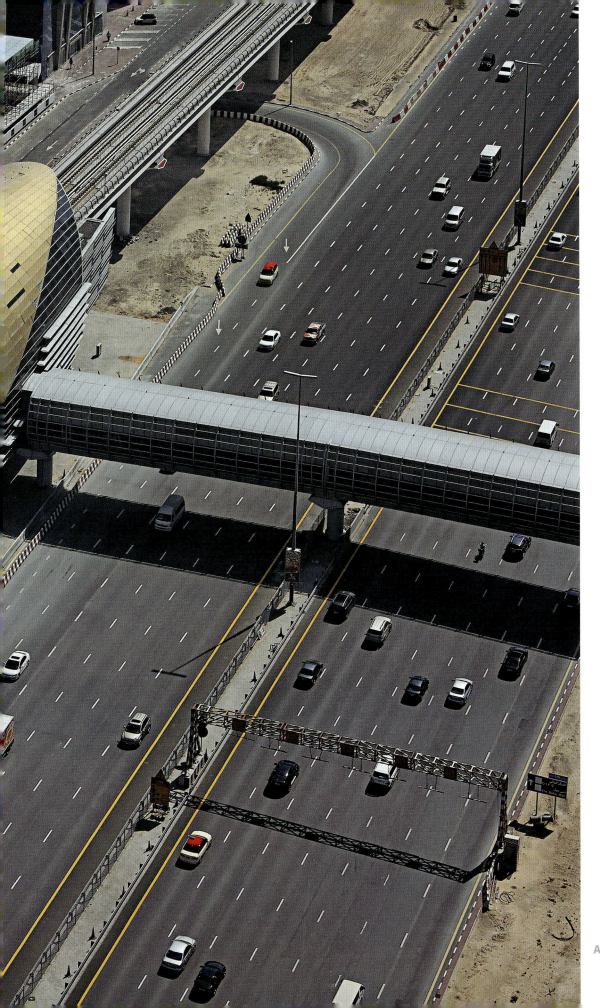

Dubai is the largest city in the United Arab Emirates; its only rail transportation system, the Dubai Metro, was built in four years. Sections were opened in September 2009. The Metro connects Dubai International Airport with the city center (Red Line); after further expansion, this will be followed by a connection to Dubai World Central International Airport. The second central line, linking the districts of Deira and Bur Dubai (Green Line), opened in September 2011 with sixteen new stations and 23 km of tracks. In autumn 2010, the UAE transport authority reported that public transport accounted for 11 percent of total traffic.

Dubai—United Arab Emirates

The Financial Center train station is a state-of-the-art structure on the Dubai Metro Red Line. The rapid-transit station opened in 2009 and has two side platforms, which are covered by a futuristic train shed. The city's subway network is called the Dubai Metro and is the fourth subway network in the Middle East region. It opened in 2009 and operates entirely as an automated driverless system running on a network of 1,435 mm standard-gauge lines. The eighty-seven Dubai Metro trains are driverless, five-section, multiple-unit train sets 85 m long. Delivered by the Japanese company Kinki Sharyō, they are numbered 5001–5087 and powered by a power rail parallel to the main track.
| picture alliance / Monheim picture archive

Asia and the Middle East **133**

Bukhara—Uzbekistan

Since its independence from the Soviet Union in 1991, Uzbekistan has thoroughly modernized and expanded its railroad network. The Bukhara railroad station was restored to its former glory, as this 2017 photograph shows. The history of Bukhara railroad station goes back to the nineteenth century, when the Trans-Caspian Railroad was built through central Asia. In 1888, the railroad ran through the village of Kagan, near Bukhara. A short time later, a narrow-gauge railroad was built to the city and later replaced by the broad-gauge railroad. Today's Bukhara station is in Kagan, around 10 km from the city center. It is the terminus for high-speed trains running from Tashkent to Samarkand. In July 2011, the first 250 km/hour Talgo high-speed articulated train was procured from Spain. Two more were added from 2016 to 2018, and another two trains have been ordered. The trains operate as the Afrosiyob service and reach a speed of 230 km per hour on scheduled runs.
| Julia Drugova / Shutterstock

After Uzbekistan became independent in 1991, the country's railroad network was separated from Soviet Railways. As a result, Uzbekistan Railways still essentially operates on the same parameters as the former Soviet Railways system, in particular the broad 1,520 mm gauge. The OTY (O'zbekiston temir yo'llari) Uzbekistan state railroad was founded on November 7, 1994. Independence also meant that Uzbekistan's borders with the neighboring republics became national borders. The new borders severed the former Soviet Railway lines. For this reason, Uzbekistan has expanded its rail network by around 2,500 km since independence, and an additional 1,170 km of lines have been rehabilitated and upgraded. Today, Uzbek trains can reach speeds of up to 250 km per hour. The newly built lines now avoid taking transit routes through neighboring countries. Around a third of the approximately 7,500 km network of lines is electrified. However, not only has Uzbekistan built tracks and set up poles for catenary overhead lines: sixteen passenger stations have been rebuilt since independence and fourteen have been completely renovated, including the southern station in Tashkent, the capital city.

The withdrawal of the colonial power of Great Britain from the British Raj (Hindi for "Rule") on the Indian subcontinent after World War II led to not one independent state, but two: Pakistan as well as India. Pakistan, then consisting of West and East Pakistan (now Bangladesh), united most of the predominantly Muslim-populated territories. In 1956, Pakistan ultimately proclaimed itself the first Islamic republic in the world. Even today, the railroad system is largely shaped by this British Indian past. In the past few decades, the many narrow-gauge (1 m wide) lines in Pakistan have been converted into broad gauge (1,676 mm), making it possible to take the last steam locomotives out of service by 2005. Pakistan's rather loosely knit rail network, which is about 8,000 km long, is concentrated in the densely populated provinces of Punjab and Sindh. However, the country's southwestern region, where the port city of Gwadar is located, has not yet been connected to the rail network. Besides this, it is not possible to reach the mountainous north by rail. In Pakistan, the railroad is a less important means of transport than in neighboring India.

Karachi—Pakistan

In Pakistan, the railroad is the number one means of mass transportation. On September 6, 2012, crowds were waiting on platform 2 of the Cantt (short for Cantonment) Railway Station in Karachi; their train had been delayed because of torrential rain. The port city's train station, which opened in 1898 and has been modernized several times, has five through tracks and offers travel to all parts of the country.

| picture alliance / PPI Images

Rawalpindi—Pakistan

An everyday scene at Rawalpindi Railway Station: two Pakistani men are traveling with their goats. Rawalpindi Station is one of several major stops on the Karachi–Peshawar railroad line. It opened in 1881 and has five platforms. The Pakistani railroad network is laid in broad gauge (1,676 mm), and all of the original narrow-gauge railroad lines have been converted to broad gauge or closed down in recent decades.

| picture alliance / AA

Asia and the Middle East **135**

Mumbai—India

The Chhatrapati Shivaji Maharaj Terminus, also called Mumbai CST, and until 1996 known as Victoria Terminus, is a station of Indian Railways in the southern part of Mumbai. It is one of the largest and busiest railroad stations in the world and has been designated a UNESCO World Heritage Site since 2004. In 1878, British architect Frederick William Stevens (1847–1900) was commissioned to design a train station building as the western terminal station for long-distance rail service to and from the port city, then called Bombay. He drew inspiration from London's St Pancras Station. When the building was completed in 1888, it was considered the largest and most important building in British India. It is designed in Victorian neo-Gothic style and draws few stylistic elements from Indo-Islamic architecture, in contrast to other contemporaneous or later imposing buildings of British India under the Raj. The platforms, covered with a steel-and-glass roof, are between 200 and 700 m long. Above the main entrance rises an octagonal dome about 100 m high, supported by a ribbed structure and accessible on foot. In the interior are open porticoes. The building is richly decorated with stone sculptures and reliefs. The standing figure of the Lady of Progress rises atop the dome. | picture alliance / robertharding

Endlessly long passenger trains, travelers clinging to the outside of the rail carriages or riding on the roof or the locomotive, train stations besieged by beggars and day laborers—these are the associations that come to mind when you think of India's railroads. The first railroad in India ran from Bombay to Tane, 33 km away, starting in 1853. The gauge was 1,675 mm (5 feet, 6 inches), which was later designated the Indian broad gauge and is used for most of the long-distance railroad lines on the Indian subcontinent. This and other railroads were first built and operated by British-controlled companies. The railroad network in British India comprised approximately 40,000 km of rail lines. In 1947, after independence from the United Kingdom and the division of the former colonial territory into the nations of India and Pakistan, the railroad network also had to be divided. In 1951, the various railroad companies merged to form the current structure of Indian Railways. Today India has the fourth-largest rail network in the world, after the United States, China, and Russia. In March 2017, it comprised more than 67,000 km of track, of which 61,700 km were broad-gauge lines, 3,500 km were meter-gauge lines, and 2,200 km were the even-narrower Indian narrow-gauge lines. Of the broad-gauge lines, 22,000 km were double-tracked and 25,400 km were electrified, representing 38 percent of the network. The network serves 7,349 railroad stations, from simple stops to grandiose colonial-style terminal stations.

Mumbai—India

View into one of the train sheds of the Chhatrapati Shivaji Terminus (formerly Victoria Terminus) in Mumbai, India, with arriving local trains. The long exposure creates a diffuse representation of the stream of commuters leaving their trains. | picture alliance / robertharding

New Delhi—India

Train platform scene from New Delhi, with a helpful vendor selling chips, cookies, and water. Given the long traveling times in India, this type of food service will exist for a long time to come. In the background is a "sleeper-class" car, the cheapest sleeping-car category in India. This is a non-air-conditioned couchette car with six-bed compartments on one side of the aisle, and two beds—one atop the other—along the length of the car on the other side. There are no curtains between the aisle and the beds, and the windows are barred for safety. | Natasha Karpuk / Shutterstock

Asia and the Middle East **137**

Jalgaon—India

Everyday service at the train station in Jalgaon. At the front of the train is one of 778 examples of the WAP-4 series of electric locomotives built at India's domestic Chittaranjan Locomotive Works (CLW); these locomotives started service between 1993 and 2016. Jalgaon has roughly half a million inhabitants. It is located in the state of Maharashta and offers good rail connections. From Jalgaon Junction Station one can travel in the direction of Mumbai, Nagpur, or Delhi.

| Leonid Andronov / Shutterstock

Kuala Lumpur—Malaysia

The old train station in Kuala Lumpur, the capital of Malaysia, is a genuinely magnificent building. After the city was given a new central station in 2001, only trains offering local service stop at the old station. The Victorian-Moorish-style station was built in 1910–1911. Today it is used as a six-star hotel.
| picture alliance / imageBROKER

Malaysia, a monarchy with thirteen million inhabitants, is in Southeast Asia. It is a federation of thirteen states. These include West Malaysia—where the capital city of Kuala Lumpur is located—on the Malay Peninsula, and East Malaysia, which occupies part of the island of Borneo. The South China Sea lies between the two roughly equal parts of the country. As a result, Malaysia has two separate railroad networks. The country's rail infrastructure covers 1,792 km of tracks. Of this, 1,735 km are in the 1 m (narrow) gauge that was historically laid in Malaysia, and 57 km are laid in the standard gauge of 1,435 mm. The greatest part of the network runs on the mainland and is operated by the Keretapi Tanah Melayu (Malayan Railways Ltd.). About 207 km of the lines are electrified.

A double-tracked new line from Kuala Lumpur to the city of Ipoh, designed for a top speed of 160 km per hour, was completed in early 2008. North of Ipoh, a line is currently being built to the town of Padang Besar, which lies near the border with Thailand. There is already cross-border rail service to Thailand and Singapore. Beyond this, there is also the Keretapi Negeri Sabah, the Sabah State Railway Department, which operates a 134 km long line with a meter-wide gauge on Borneo.

Ipoh—Malaysia

Ipoh is the capital of the Malaysian state of Perak and boasts a truly beautiful train station. Designed as a hospital at the beginning of the twentieth century, it is affectionately called the "Taj Mahal." The opening was planned for 1917—but then came World War I, and the plans by British architect Arthur Benison Hubback were put on hold. The railroad station, built in the neo-Moorish/Mughal/Indo-Saracenic styles, did not open until 1935. | Syarif Hidayatullah / Shutterstock

Asia and the Middle East **141**

Đà Lat—Vietnam

This railroad station is one of the sights of Đà Lat, a large city in the highlands of South Vietnam. The art deco station building was designed 1932 by French architects Moncet and Reveron and opened in 1938. The Tháp Chàm–Đà Lat line was an 84 km long, narrow-gauge (1 m) railroad line that connected Đà Lat with the country's north–south railroad. The line opened in 1932. Operations were suspended in 1968, after Vietcong forces attacked the rail line during the Vietnam War. In the 1990s, the 7 km section between Đà Lat and Trai Mát was rebuilt as a tourist attraction. Trains run on this route under the name of the "Dalat Plateau Railroad." Incidentally, two of the original steam locomotives now run on the heritage Furka Steam Railway in Switzerland.

| picture alliance / imageBROKER

The history of railroads in Vietnam was initially marked by the colonial policy of the French Republic in what was then French Indochina, and later by the decades-long wars under which Vietnam suffered. After Vietnam was reunited in 1975, the North Vietnamese State Railways took over the facilities and rolling stock in South Vietnam. Everything was badly damaged, both in the South and in the North. Repair work began immediately. It was possible to do this only by closing down other railroad lines and reusing the materials. Today, the network includes 2,437 km of rail lines and 3,159 km of tracks, including the passing sidings and tracks inside the train stations. None of the lines are electrified, and all are single track.

In Thailand, construction of railroad lines began in 1892. At that time, the country needed a means of transportation that would allow it to move troops and materials rapidly in the event of an invasion by a colonial power. Today, the State Railway of Thailand (SRT) operates a narrow-gauge rail network more than 4,400 km long. The lines start from the capital city Bangkok, running in all directions like the five points of a star. However, the SRT is not exactly successful. The number of travelers—passenger trains offer three classes of rail carriage—is low. The railroads' share of the transport market is only 6 percent. The situation is even worse for freight transport, where it amounts to only 2 percent. This is due to the high prices and outdated materials. Modernizing the network, expanding the double-tracked sections, acquiring better rolling stock, increasing the average speed, and improving safety would cost around fifteen billion euros ($18 billion) over the coming years. The government had decided in principle at the end of 2009 to make the necessary investments, but so far these words have been followed by little action.

Bangkok—Thailand

The Thai metropolis, with its millions of inhabitants, relies on the railroad as an environmentally friendly means of mass transportation. This aerial photograph from November 11, 2018, shows the Bang Sue Grand central station, which is under construction and due to open soon. Bang Sue Central Station is built on several levels. An underground garage will offer space for 1,700 vehicles, and the ticket counter, a large passenger lounge, and shops will be on the ground level. There are four platforms for local trains and eight for long-distance trains on the first level. Ten more are available on the second level of this mega train station, to accommodate regional service as well as the trains of planned high-speed connections and the Airport Rail Link. | Zephyr_p/Shutterstock

Nabon—Thailand

A countryside railroad station in Thailand. Nabon is the name of the train station in the Amphon Na Bon district in Nakhon Si Thammarat Province. Here, the long-distance train to Bangkok is ready for departure on the Southern Line, pulled by an SRT-series, six-axle, diesel-electric state railroad locomotive.
| Pratan Saetang / Shutterstock

Asia and the Middle East **145**

Tang Gu La—Chinese Tibet Border

A Chinese worker stands next to the sign for Tang Gu La, a new train station on the new Qinghai–Tibet Railroad line. The Tang Gu La train station is located on the Tibetan border with Qinghai Province, China, at an altitude of 5,068 m above sea level, making it the train station at the highest elevation in the world.
| picture alliance / dpa

Hsinchu—Taiwan

Hsinchu is a city in the northwestern part of the Republic of China on Taiwan, with just under half a million inhabitants. The Hsinchu Railroad Station was built during the Japanese occupation of Taiwan, which lasted from 1895 to 1945. The station's importance has diminished in recent years, since the trains on the high-speed line from Nankang district in southern Taipei, the capital city, to Zuoying city, which started service in 2007, stop at a new station outside Hsinchu. In 2011, however, a feeder line opened that connects the two train stations in Hsinchu.
| Richie Chan / Shutterstock

Changhua—Taiwan

Classic rail yards—or depots—look the same all over the world. This aerial photograph shows the Changhua city rail yard in Taiwan. The locomotives are distributed on a turntable to the stalls in the semicircular roundhouse, and additional dead-end tracks in the open serve as parking places for other locomotives. That was how things were done during the steam engine era, and it is the same today as systems are modernized. The coaling system has long since been replaced by two oil tanks that store fuel for the many diesel locomotives.
| elwynn/Shutterstock

The rail networks in Taiwan, Republic of China, comprise a total length of 1,841 km (as of 2007). All the railroad lines are on the island of Taiwan; there are no railroads on the smaller islands that are part of the Republic of China. The Taiwan Railway Administration (TRA) manages a 1,097 km long conventional rail network on tracks with a narrow 1,067 mm gauge. Beyond this, a 345 km, high-speed, standard-gauge line has been running between Taipei and the port of Kaohsiung since 2007. The cities of Taipei and Kaohsiung both have subway systems. The 86 km long Alishan Forest Railway and the Sugar Railways in Taiwan are narrow railroads with 762 mm wide gauge originally built to transport freight; now they carry mostly tourists.

No country in the world has invested as much in rail transport during the last few decades as the People's Republic of China. One high-speed line after another has been built at an almost sensational pace, while at the same time modernization of the rolling stock was propelled forward. Although steam locomotives were still being built in 1988, the China State Railroad was able to celebrate the turn of the millennium "steam free." When the People's Republic of China was founded in 1949, the railroad network consisted of around 22,000 km of tracks, about half of which had been destroyed during the previous years of war. About half of the provincial capital cities had no rail connection to Beijing. The rail network was expanded slowly and had reached about 54,000 km by the first half of the 1990s, of which 11,200 km were double-tracked and 6,500 km were electrified. Although the rail network was severely underdeveloped given the size of the country, it carried 71 percent of all the passengers and 56 percent of all freight. In view of the major bottlenecks, investments have been made in rail infrastructure and rolling stock since the turn of the millennium. The railroads, which are the main long-distance mode of transport in China, were able to run on 120,970 km of tracks by 2016. Between 2008 and 2018, China built the largest high-speed rail network in the world, with lines totaling 29,000 km long. Another milestone was the opening of the Qinghai–Tibet Railroad, or Lhasa Express, in 2006. This railroad line, which is almost 2,000 km long, stops at Tang Gu La, the highest-elevation train station in the world at 5,068 m above sea level. A quarter of the line runs over permafrost soil; for climatic reasons, the ground is cooled during the warmer seasons to prevent it from thawing.

Asia and the Middle East

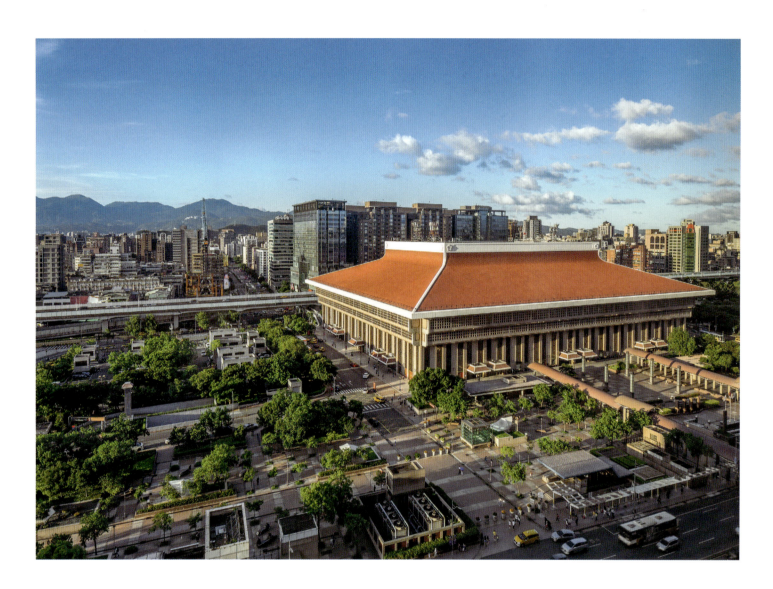

Taipei—Taiwan

Taipei Main Station, which opened in 1897, is a rail hub in Taiwan, the capital of the Republic of China. This modern rail transport structure opened in 1989. It is used for local and long-distance traffic and has twenty-four station tracks with platforms. The station is operated by the Taiwan Railway Administration, Taipei Rapid-Transit Corporation, and Taiwan High-Speed Rail. The greater part of the track system is underground. The station has been connected to the Taiwanese high-speed network since 2007.
| Richie Chan / Shutterstock

Harbin—China

Harbin is an important railway junction in northeastern China. This photograph shows an everyday scene with a high-speed train in the main railroad station, one of four train stations in the city. The station opened in 1899 and was expanded and modernized in 1999. | ZDL/Shutterstock

Beijing—China

The development of the railroads in China is fascinating: a good thirty years ago, the Chinese were still manufacturing steam locomotives; today the country has by far the largest high-speed rail network in the world. The Beijing South Railway Station fits into this picture. Opened on August 1, 2008, in the run-up to the Olympic Games that year, it links the Beijing metropolitan area to the high-speed rail network running to the south. Designed by British architect Terry Farrell in collaboration with the Tianjin Design Institute, the station replaced the former Yongdingmen South Station after less than three years in construction. A characteristic feature of Beijing South Station is the terminal building concourse, with its elliptical roof 500 m wide and 380 m long. The terminal building accommodates the waiting room, which extends across the tracks and provides access to the twenty-four platforms. The station takes up an area of 420,000 m², making it the third-largest railroad station in China. The station building accounts for 310,000 m² of that area.

| picture alliance / Photoshot

Shanghai—China

State-of-the-art architecture characterizes Shanghai's South Railway Station. This aerial photograph shows the roof of the first railroad station in the world to feature a circular station building elevated above the tracks. The train station, which opened in 2006, is one of the four most important train stations in Shanghai and provides service primarily to China's southern provinces.
| M. Scheja / Shutterstock

Hangzhuo—China

Even on modern railroads, not much can be done without the staff. A friendly train attendant looks out the door of a G85 high-speed train in Hangzhou, en route from Shanghai to Guangzhou in December 2014. Service started on this high-speed line a few days earlier.
| picture alliance / Photoshot-neoclassical

Tokyo—Japan

Japan is one of the most densely populated countries on Earth. This is demonstrated in this aerial photograph of Tokyo; a sea of houses surrounds the railroad lines. Train-marshaling yards are almost exclusively located outside the big cities. | marchello74/Shutterstock

The national railroads railway of the fourth-largest island nation in the world—Japan comprises a total of 6,852 islands of various sizes—is considered a pioneer of high-speed transport on the rails. Both the standard-gauge, high-speed lines and the multiple-unit trains, which ushered in a new era of rail transport in Japan in 1964, are called the Shinkansen ("new main line"). While the first Shinkansen trains ran at a speed of 220 km per hour, today they reach 320 km per hour on scheduled runs. Today the Japanese railroads have been privatized and have a dense network on the most-important islands. In Japan, the tracks for general passenger and freight service are laid in Cape gauge—a narrow, 1,067 mm wide gauge: this network encompasses 22,207 km of tracks, of which 15,430 km are electrified. The high-speed lines and some suburban lines are built in the standard gauge of 1,435 mm; this network is 4,800 km long, all of which are electrified. As a side note, some of the lines are laid out in the Scottish gauge (1,372 mm) and in the very narrow 762 mm gauge.

Asia and the Middle East **153**

Tokyo—Japan

The Western influence on Japan is reflected at Tokyo Central Station, built in 1914. Tokyo Station is located in the Chiyoda city ward of Marunouchi commercial district, not far from the Imperial Palace and just north of the Ginza district. In addition to the Shinkansen lines, many urban rapid-transit and regional train lines, as well as the Marunouchi Line subway line, cross here. Unusual for a major Japanese station is the lack of private rail lines. However, these terminate at the outskirts. An underground passage connects it to the nearby Otemachi subway station. The modern high-rise buildings in the background create an attractive backdrop. | Peera_stockfoto/Shutterstock

Tokyo—Japan

Nocturnal platform scene in Shinjuku Station, a Tokyo urban rapid-transit station. Shinjuku is known as a nightlife district featuring clubs, bars, restaurants, karaoke, and the red-light district. Shinjuku Station is the busiest station in the world, used by about 3.5 million passengers a day. There are lot of people waiting for the last Yamanote, Tokyo's circular (or loop) urban rapid-transit line. The line is 34.5 km long; the trains run on Cape gauge (1,067 mm), and the maximum speed is 90 km per hour. | picture alliance / dpa

Asia and the Middle East **155**

Tokyo—Japan

Tokyo Station is the main train station in the Japanese capital city, and the starting point for almost all the Shinkansen lines. The most important section of the station consists of ten platforms on a viaduct, which run in a north–south direction. The main entrance is on the west side of the station in the historic station building facing the Imperial Palace. The station building, which was opened in 1914, can be seen at the left edge of the photo. The station concourse runs the entire width of the structure and has access to the other tunnel complexes on all sides. | MAHATHIR MOHD YASIN / Shutterstock

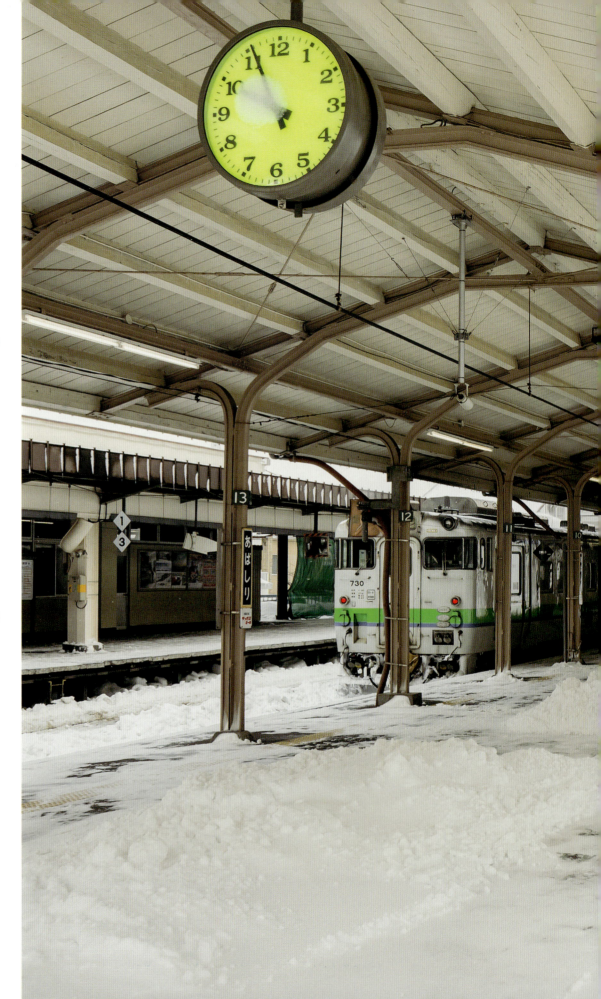

Abashiri—Japan

Abashiri Station, which opened in 1912, is located in the western Shinmachi district of this city on Hokkaido, Japan's second-largest island and northernmost prefecture. The station is oriented from west to east and has five tracks, three of which are used for passenger service. These are located next to the platform at the station building and a canopied central, or island, platform connected to the station building on the north side of the facility via a covered overpass. From an operational point of view, this is a terminal station accessible from both sides: the trains switch from one line to the other only rarely, since Abashiri is almost always the terminus for the line. Express trains to Sapporo leave from the station building platform.
| TwoKim studio / Shutterstock

158

IV. AUSTRALIA AND NEW ZEALAND—MORE THAN JUST *LORD OF THE RINGS* AND KOALAS

The Australian railroad is famous for having the longest run of straight tracks in the world: 478 km, part of the 1,692 km long Trans-Australian Railway, which runs from the city of Kalgoorlie to Port Augusta. In 1854, Melbourne's first steam train started running between the city center and the port of Melbourne. During the period that followed, many private companies were involved in building and operating Australia's railroad lines. When the federation was formed in 1901, trains were running on three different gauges, making it difficult to operate the railroads. Only since around 1970 has it been possible to take a continuous trip from Sydney to Perth, on the West Coast, without having to change from one rail system to another. Part of this trip is made on mixed-gauge tracks (three rails). The total length of the national railroad network is around 34,000 km. The length of the privately operated rail network is around 5,500 km. Private rail networks are used in the Pilbara region of the state of Western Australia, primarily for transporting iron ore, and in the state of Queensland, for transporting coal and sugar cane. Compared with road traffic, passenger and freight transport by rail now plays a subordinate role. The Sydney-to-Perth Trans-Australian Railroad is important for freight and tourism service. The few long-distance trains are particularly important for tourism. In the metropolitan areas of Brisbane, Melbourne, Perth, and Sydney, where half the population lives, there are well-developed urban rapid-transit networks.

Brisbane—Australia

A bird's-eye view of Brisbane, Australia, including its through-transport railroad station. The capital city of the state of Queensland has more than two million inhabitants. Brisbane is on the Sydney–Cairns main line, and a route branches off toward the city of Toowoomba. Australian railroads are of little importance for long-distance travel, but local public transport is flourishing. The Airtrain, which provides a connection to Brisbane's international airport, is popular. | picture alliance / Reinhard Dirscherl

Melbourne—Australia

This 2014 photo shows Flinders Street Railway Station, the most important public transport hub in the capital city of Victoria. The station building is on the corner of Flinders Street and Swanston Street, and the Yarra River flows by the track and platform facilities in the back. The entrance area is at street level and one level higher than the rail facilities, which could have been designed as a through station at the lower level. Since starting service in 1910, the station has been modernized several times and today has fourteen tracks with platforms. The characteristic domed structure is the main entrance to the station. A protected historic landmark, it is probably the most photographed building in town. Platform 1 is 708 m long, making it the fourth-longest platform in the world. At least, that's what the Australian government says.
| ChameleonsEye/Shutterstock

Melbourne—Australia

The Southern Cross Railway Station, built between 2002 and 2006, features an innovative, trapezoidal roof. The structure spans an area of 216 by 180 m and has a complex geometry with no symmetry or repetition. Southern Cross is Melbourne's most important long-distance train station, but this through station, with fifteen station tracks with platforms, also serves local trains. Two tracks are multigauge and can be used both by standard-gauge and broad-gauge trains. | picture alliance / Reinhard Koester

Oamaru—New Zealand

Oamaru is a small town in the Waitaki District in Otago Region on the South Island. Its many historic buildings make it a popular tourist destination. Oamaru is connected to the South Island's Main Trunk Railway, also called the Main South Line, and freight traffic runs here regularly. Passenger service was discontinued in 2002, when the "Southerner" train stopped running. Today, the Oamaru Steam and Railway Society heritage railroad, which runs on the tracks of the former port, commemorates the great age of the railroad.
| Naruedom Yaempongsa / Shutterstock

Dunedin—New Zealand

The platform of the historical station building at Dunedin, on the South Island of New Zealand, appears deserted. The state-owned New Zealand Rail and its successor, the privatized Tranz Rail and Toll Rail, respectively, have shut down their passenger service, but this continues to be a working railroad station; the Otago Excursion Train Trust has been using the Flemish Renaissance–style station since 1990. It is the most important tourist railroad in the country, and trips begin here.
| picture alliance / imageBROKER

In the second half of the nineteenth century, there was a veritable railroad boom on New Zealand's two largest islands, which led to the construction of main and branch lines that were largely built in Cape gauge. One hundred years later, things were looking very different: many of the branch lines had been shut down, the main lines lost their second tracks, and even electrification was reversed. Rail service had been privatized in recent years, but the network is now back in the hands of the government. Freight traffic is transported mostly in block trains, which carry bulk commodities. Long-distance passenger service is limited to only four pairs of trains that are important mostly for tourism; additionally, extensive local train service operates in the metropolitan areas around Wellington and Auckland. Many museums and heritage railroads recall the "old railroads." There are also special steam locomotive trips that run on the nationalized railroad tracks, which are enjoying ever-greater popularity.

Wellington—New Zealand

This partial view of Wellington shows not only the Westpac Stadium, but also the railroad station's extensive system of tracks. In 1908, Wellington got its first railroad, which was in Cape gauge (1,076 mm). After intermittent privatizations, it reverted to government hands when the Toll Rail company was nationalized and renamed Kiwi Rail. Kiwi Rail operates all passenger rail services in New Zealand. | picture alliance / AFKersting / akg-images